Discourse Perspectives on Syntax

EDITED BY

Flora Klein-Andreu

Research Department
Center for Applied Linguistics
Washington D.C.

ACADEMIC PRESS

A Subsidiary of Harcourt Brace Jovanovich, Publishers
New York   London
Paris   San Diego   San Francisco   São Paulo   Sydney   Tokyo   Toronto

ACADEMIC PRESS, INC.
111 Fifth Avenue, New York, New York 10003

United Kingdom Edition published by
ACADEMIC PRESS, INC. (LONDON) LTD.
24/28 Oval Road, London NW1 7DX

B. 224097.

Library of Congress Cataloging in Publication Data
Main entry under title:

Discourse perspectives in syntax.

Includes index.
1. Discourse analysis--Addresses, essays,
lectures. 2. Grammar, Comparative and general--
Syntax--Addresses, essays, lectures. 3. Linguistic
analysis (Linguistics)--Addresses, essays, lectures.
I. Klein-Andreu, Flora.
P302.D549   1983   401.41   83-2812
ISBN 0-12-413720-2

PRINTED IN THE UNITED STATES OF AMERICA

83 84 85 86   9 8 7 6 5 4 3 2 1

Contents

PART I
Events in Discourse

1

Relative Tense in Discourse: The Inference of Time
Orientation in Swahili   3
ELLEN CONTINI-MORAVA

2

The Discourse Function of the Participle in Ancient Greek 23
BARBARA A. FOX

3

Grammar and Discourse: The English Detached Participial Clause 43
SANDRA A. THOMPSON

4

Ergative, Passive, and Active in Malay Narrative 67
PAUL J. HOPPER

PART II
Entities in Discourse

5

Referents and Topic within and across Discourse Units: Observations from Current Vernacular English

BENJI WALD

6

On the Interaction of Word Order and Intonation: Some OV Constructions in Spanish

CARMEN SILVA-CORVALÁN

CHAPTER THREE

Grammar and Discourse: The English Detached Participial Clause

Sandra A. Thompson

1. Introduction

Sentences such as (1) are common in certain varieties of written English:

(1)   *The Spanish infantry desperately hurled themselves against the palisades,* **hacking at the logs with axes.**

The boldfaced clause in this sentence is an example of a present participial "absolute" clause (hereafter simply DETACHED PARTICIPLE) whose function in English discourse is the focus of this study.

The detached participle can be contrasted with several other types of present participial (i.e., *-ing*) constructions. The detached participle is the only *-ing* construction in English that is "detached." The term "detached" I take from the tradition of Russian grammar as described by Rappaport (1979), where intonational criteria are used to distinguish "detached" and "nondetached" constituents. For English, I would suggest that a working definition of "detached clause" include the criteria of being set off by pauses, of exhibiting a clause-final falling intonation contour characteristic of independent clauses, or of being preceded by a clause ending with a clause-final falling contour. These intonational signals of detachment are virtually without exception marked by commas in writing.

This notion of detachment, then, permits a distinction between detached participles and all of the following uses of *-ing* forms, about which I shall have nothing further to say:

a. Relative clauses
   *The woman **standing** in the corner is my boss.*
b. Complement to *there is*
   *There's a guy **picking** pears.*
c. Complements to verbs of perception
   *She sees them **walking** away.*
d. Complements to "phase" verbs
   *They start **eating** them.*
   *They keep **walking** back.*
   *He was busy **cleaning** his desk.*
e. Complements to verbs of "appearance"
   *She just stood there **staring** at me.*
   *He came in **limping**.*
   *She went **riding** past the tree.*
f. Combined with BE in a progressive
   *They're all **standing** around.*
   *We couldn't figure out what was **happening**.*
g. Prenominal modifier
   *What will you do with the two **remaining** avocados?*
h. Gerunds
   *He thanked the boys for **helping** him.*
   *Cats don't like **getting** wet.*

Also excluded from consideration here are participial forms in clauses beginning with the subordinators *after, before, by, with, without, while,* and *in.*

The detached participle, I suggest, can be characterized in the following way:

1. It serves as a device that allows the speaker/writer to present certain material as background against which certain other material can be put forth as "figure" in the Gestalt sense. That is, the detached participle is not just background, but it is background specifically for the "main" clause with which it is associated. By "background," I mean material that serves to further explicate, amplify, or elaborate what is in the main clause, or that represents an event occurring simultaneously with or providing a comment on or motivation for the event in the main clause. In (1), for example, the detached participle *hacking at the logs with axes* provides a detail that functions to amplify and elaborate the report that the infantry hurled themselves against the palisades. A clause so backgrounded refuses, as it were, to allow the exposition to advance while some ancillary material is presented.

2. This background material is furthermore presented as "pure" back-

ground, with no explicit relationship being designated to hold between it and the material that forms the figure.

The second fact, that the detached participle does not explicitly express any logical or temporal relationship with the material for which it is the background, predicts the detached participle's distribution in discourse, which is the focus of Section 2.

The first fact, that the detached participle provides background of a very local sort, predicts a certain set of grammatical properties, which is the subject matter of Section 3.

2. Distribution in Discourse

The first point to make about the occurrence of the detached participle in discourse is that, as is intuitively obvious to anyone who knows English, and as is noted by Jespersen (1933:313), it is found much more commonly in formal written than in informal spoken English. To substantiate this intuition, I studied the 35 pages of transcribed informal adult speech in Carterette and Jones (1974), and found only one instance of a detached participle, the boldfaced clause in the following sentence:[1]

(2)   *But wouldn't you feel as though you were just you were blind and you were a nuisance to everybody around you and you were just living in a fantasy world* **pretending that you knew how to dance and pretending that you could see things.**   (p. 414)

That is a frequency of 1 instance per (roughly) 15,050 words. Just for comparison, Severin's *Explorers of the Mississippi* (1967), a rich source of detached participles, averages 111 instances per 15,050 words.

Even in descriptive monologues, which are not conversational and might be thought more closely to resemble written English, the detached participle is relatively rare. In Chafe's (1980) transcriptions of 20 narratives describing a short film about a man and his pears, a total of roughly 16,800 words, there are only 26 occurrences, of which (3) is one example:

(3)   *And he sort of* [.75] */visually/* [.25] *counts them with his fingers.* [2.95 [.8] *A — nd* [1.6]] *leans back up against the tree,* [1.2] *I*

---

[1] There are unsatisfactory aspects of Carterette and Jones' transcriptions as a data source, the most glaring of which is the failure to indicate both intonation and to which of several participants a given utterance is to be attributed. In addition, the conversational setting is artificial. As these defects do not bear on the representation of detached participle constructions, however, I judged this corpus to be a reasonable reflection of their frequency in spoken English.

> guess, [.55] *wondering . . . what happened to [1.3] the missing basket* (p. 306).[2]

Thus the detached participle clearly seems to be characteristic of literary, rather than conversational, English. A possible explanation for this will be proposed in what follows. For now, I note this fact as justification for considering only written discourse from here on.

Turning now to the distribution of the detached participle in written English, we might recall the characterization given in Section 1, in which the detached participle was described as "ground" for material that is intended to be taken as "figure." The figure–ground metaphor allows us to identify a detached participle in relation to a "main" clause. We can then say that the detached participle is used to provide "local" background, that is, background for the main clause (see Fox, this volume, for a characterization of the participle in ancient Greek discourse in exactly the same terms). The way in which it does this, however, is "with no strings attached": It can be used only when no explicit connection, either temporal or logical, is being drawn between the background material and the figure material.

The implications of this fact are clear: The detached participle is most compatible with a discourse whose purpose is to describe events rather than to state temporal or logical relationships among them. We would expect, then, that descriptive discourse would be high in frequency of detached participles, whereas discourse whose primary function is nondescriptive exposition would contain relatively few instances. This is precisely what we find.

In fact, the type of discourse in which detached participles abound can be characterized with even greater precision: It is discourse that attempts to describe by creating an image. To this function the detached participle is well suited, precisely because of its unspecified relationship with the main clause. For discourse purporting to evoke an image, I use the term DEPICTIVE.[3]

To illustrate the contrast between depictive and nondepictive discourse, we can compare texts for average number of detached participles per 10,000 words. The differences are dramatic. As mentioned, one of the richest of the

[2] The relevant transcription conventions are:
  . sentence-final falling intonation
  , clause-final but not sentence-final intonation
  /X/ X may not be an accurate transcription
  — lengthened segment
  . . . break in timing too short to be measured as pause
  [X] pause lasting X seconds
  [X[Y] a-nd u-m [Z]] a sequence lasting a total of X seconds, consisting of a pause of Y seconds, a-nd u-m, and a pause of Z seconds (p. 301).

[3] My appreciation to R. McMillan Thompson for suggesting this term.

texts examined was Severin's *Explorers of the Mississippi*. This text is a detailed historical account of the early explorations of the Mississippi River, beginning with the exploits of Hernando de Soto in the mid-sixteenth century. Here is a typical paragraph, which gives a flavor of the depictive style — note that there are three detached participles in this paragraph alone:

(4)   *De Soto's life was saved but his negligence was still to provide the*
       ruin of his expedition. During the skirmish in the town, the
       Indians in the baggage train had seized their opportunity to escape.
       They broke ranks and streamed into Mobila, **taking with them all**
       the Spanish supplies including the spare weapons, sacraments,
       tents, pearls, and gunpowder. *By the time the main body of the*
       Spanish army arrived, the situation was desperate. They had only
       their weapons, while on the other side of Mobila's palisades lay all
       the equipment they needed to survive the march down the coast.
       Already the ramparts were lined with newly-liberated slaves,
       jeering *and* **holding up their booty to mock the white men.**   (p. 38)

In *Explorers of the Mississippi*, there are an average of 74 detached participles per 10,000 words. At the opposite end of the scale is a book such as Goth's *Medical Pharmacology*, in which 10,000 words yields only 5 detached participles. The striking difference between these two texts in frequency of detached participles is an accurate illustration of the tendency for these clauses to occur in depictive genres.

Another way of illustrating this contrast is to compare depictive and nondepictive portions of the same text. An article from the "soft news" pullout section of the *Christian Science Monitor* entitled "Coal: Report from Mine No. 7" (April 15, 1981 Reprinted by permission from the Christian Science Monitor. © 1981 The Christian Science Publishing Society. All rights reserved.) provides an ideal text for such a comparison. This article contains approximately 2630 words (apart from quoted speech). The correspondent's stated purpose in undertaking the research for the article is summed up in this paragraph:

(5)   *I have come to West Virginia to explore the coalfields and try to*
       understand what, besides good money, attracts these workers to the
       perils and discomfort of labor in tunnels sunk beneath tree-capped
       mountains of rock.

For our purposes, what is interesting about this article is the concentration of detached participles in the purely depictive portions, as compared to the "fact-providing" portions. The first third of the article (121 lines out of 277) provides background information on mining and miners, and contains a single detached participle. Here are three representative passages:

(6)　*Here in these rich fields of high-volatility, low-sulfur bituminous coal, "drift" mines (drilled horizontally into the side of a mountain) are more common than shaft mines (sunk vertically into the earth). Either way, the mines are identical, once you get inside.*

(7)　*In case of a mine disaster, he tells me, I am to pull open the respirator immediately and put the breathing apparatus into my mouth. It might burn my lips, he warns, but I am to keep using it anyway, since it's better to have burned lips than breathe poison gas.*

(8)　*At distant reaches of the mine, a mechanical behemoth known as "the longwall" is chomping away at the coal, **causing what sounds like a dull roar at this distance.***

　　It was the longwall that led mining companies to ask for seven-day work schedules, in order to keep the machine running continuously so it would pay for itself. And it was the longwall that attracted me to No. 7, since here they're using what is considered the largest, most spectacular, and most productive piece of equipment in modern mining.

The writer then shifts from this fact-presenting mode into a much more image-creating one, and here the detached participles flourish: In 65 lines (half the number of lines in the initial selection, which had one detached participle), there are seven occurrences. The passages in (9) and (10) contain three examples:

(9)　***Howling mournfully, staring ahead with two eyelike headlights,*** *a giant mechanical insect lumbers into view. It is the continuous miner, as long as perhaps two full-size automobiles and a bit taller. But down in this cramped, subterranean world, it seems more formidable, especially with its huge rotor drum — covered with 130 steel teeth — coming at us.*

(10)　*In the far distance, through this haze, I can see the bobbing headlamps of unknown workers. **Walking to meet them,** we find two young miners who are waiting for the machine to carve out another section of the seam, so that they can go to work behind it.*

Then the content shifts again, this time away from the "scene" in the mine to the question of what attracts miners to this profession. For the next 33 lines, we find paragraphs such as these, in which there is only one detached participle:

(11)　*Through 50 years of labor–management wars, union miners have won concession after concession from coal companies, which makes union mining probably the highest-paid blue-collar job in the country, **paying $20,000 to $30,000 a year.** . . .*

[48]

> *These gains have cost the miners much, both in lost working time during strikes and in erosion of the union's power. During the past decade, the amount of coal produced under United Mine Workers contract has fallen from 70 percent of the nation's annual production to only 44 percent. And the nonunion gains worry these miners. . . .*
>
> *In this area of the country, the smaller, nonunion family-owned mines are the envy of the industry. "They may not adhere to all the safety practices the union wants," one 40-year veteran of the mines who is in management told me, "but those same mines make our productivity records look sick."*

Finally, the last 65 lines take us back into the mine itself, and, again, the detached participles blossom. The last section contains eight detached participles, of which the two in the following passage are typical:

(12)   *Just beyond the yellow curtain stands a mammoth armature of hydraulic lifts, **gleaming silver in the pitch.** A dozen men are climbing through the machinery, **repairing a conveyor chain that is about as thick as a strong man's arm.** The machine extends as far as you can see down the tunnel, and all along it men are moving back and forth through it.*

This coal article, then, provides very strong support for the claim that detached participles are particularly well suited to function in depictive discourse.

Another text that corroborates this claim in a similar way is the draft of the methodology chapter from Mary Erbaugh's dissertation on the acquisition of Mandarin syntax. (Erbaugh 1982). This chapter describes the techniques used in eliciting data from several small children in Taipei, Taiwan. The initial two sections, containing a total of about 450 lines, are highly nondepictive. They provide information about Taiwan, its sociolinguistic situation, and its value as a research site, and they give the sociolinguistic backgrounds of the children and discuss how they were selected for the study. There are eight detached participles in these two sections, for an average of one for every 56 lines. Here is one example:

(13)   *. . . industrialization and technical development are not synonymous with westernization, **an illustration being the tape recorded sutras playing over and over in Buddhist temples.***

Next comes a short section, of only about 65 lines, which depicts the typical scene Erbaugh encountered in the homes as she collected her data. Here there are no fewer than 10 detached participles, roughly 1 for every 6.5 lines.

Here is an example containing 3 instances:

(14) *I would introduce myself to the family and to the child, then sit,* **drinking tea, and chatting mostly with the parents, not** **approaching the child very directly** *until she became used to me.*

Even this small sample provides a clear illustration of the propensity of detached participles for depictive passages.

What are some other examples of depictive writing? A travel narrative is an obvious candidate. One popular style of travel writing attempts to portray the sights and sounds of the place being depicted so vividly as to conjure up in the reader's imagination what the actual experience of them would be. Woodcock's *Asia, Gods and Cities* (c Woodcock 1966) is an example of this style; it compares favorably with *Explorers of the Mississippi* at 52 detached participles per 10,000 words. These examples are typical:

(15) *That evening we sat with two Pakistani friends,* **drinking tea and** **nibbling the peppery mutton puffs.** (p. 16)

(16) *Through this Asian Andorra strolled passengers from the liners* *and the sailors from French and American warships,* **peering** **through cameras, haggling over typewriters and** **tape-recorders.** (p. 13)

Pearl Buck is a novelist whose writing is laden with detached participles. For every 10,000 words in her *The Three Daughters of Madame Liang*, there are 62 detached participles. The sentences in (17)–(19) contain four representative examples:

(17) *She was accustomed to such awakening and she lay quietly for a* *space of time,* **considering the mood,** *for she thought of it as a* *mood,* **lacking better description,** *and yet it came, she believed,* *from outside herself—unless perhaps it was natural as she got* *older?* (p. 111)

(18) *He coughed raucously, and* **fumbling in his garments,** *he* *produced a square of tissue paper, . . .* (p. 117)

(19) *She did not hear him,* **her mind concentrating upon the sun** **slipping over the horizon.** (p. 132)

The following table summarizes the frequency of detached participles in the three texts characterized as highly depictive:

TEXT	DETACHED PARTICIPLES PER 10,000 WORDS
Explorers	74
Asia	52
Mme. Liang	62

Writing that intends to spark the visual imagination, then, tends to abound in detached participles. Herein, of course, lies one clue to explaining the very low frequency of detached participles in ordinary conversational English: Conversation simply offers relatively few opportunities for the sort of planning that produces effective and evocative depictions of scenes.

What are the characteristics of nondepictive writing, where detached participles are rare? The only essential property shared by the wide range of discourse styles that can be called nondepictive is the obvious negative one: Their communicative goals are not conducive to the leisurely scene-painting for which the highly durative, temporally noncommittal detached participle is so well suited.

News analysis and commentary, for example, is typically devoid of detached participles. The backgrounding in this kind of writing is generally aimed at characterizing participants rather than describing them (hence a large number of full and truncated relative clauses), and at providing motivation, concessive or sequentially relevant facts, and hypothetical conditions, rather than depictions of scenes. An excellent example is Robert I. Rothberg's "South Africa: A Mandate for Change" (*Christian Science Monitor,* May 8, 1981, p. 23), a piece of about 790 words. It contains no detached participles; what it does contain are a large number of other types of subordinate clauses. Reproduced here are the first three paragraphs of the article with the nondepictive background clauses appearing in boldface:

(20)   *White South Africa at last has a distinct mandate for change. The results of the recent election lead to that conclusion. But Prime Minister Pieter Botha,* **leader of the ruling National Party,** *may well think otherwise.*

    Mr. Botha called an early election in **order to reposition his party and, conceivably, to weaken white opposition within the country to his calls for domestic reform. But when he began campaigning,** *Mr. Botha employed tactics of an earlier era.* **Fearful of Afrikaner antagonism to his articulation of the need to begin reforming, and mindful of a mighty assault from the right on the National Party by the Reformed National Party (HNP) and a new Conservative Party,** *he, too, appeared to move rightward. As a result, he staked no firm claim to solid reformist ground. Indeed, at times he appeared to be disavowing the "adapt or die" slogan* **that he had so strikingly promoted in 1979 and 1980.**

    Mr. Botha and his party fought a bitter rear-guard action against the right. **Although the HNP nearly quadrupled its share of the popular vote,** *it failed to win a seat. In several key rural and mining constituencies, it came very close. The National Party's percentage share of the vote fell, since the last election in*

> *1977, from 64 percent to 53 percent; the HNP was backed by 13 percent of the voters.*

Writing in the sciences and social sciences would not appear to be fertile ground for detached participles. Indeed, an example given earlier, Goth's pharmacology textbook, logs in at only 5 detached participles per 10,000 words (as compared with *Explorers*'s 74, for example). The following are three examples:

(21)   *Even the pharmacist has very little to do with the preparation of drugs, **most of them being manufactured by large companies.*** (p. 1)

(22)   *Epinephrine acts on adenyl cyclase, **catalyzing the formation of cyclic adenylic acid.** . . .* (p. 7)

(23)   *The binding of bilirubin to albumin may be inhibited by a variety of drugs such as sulfisoxazole or salicyclates, **the freed bilirubin thereby becoming ultrafiltrable.*** (p. 20)

The evolutionary biologist Richard Alexander's *Darwinism and Human Affairs* shows a comparable ratio: 8.5 detached participles per 10,000 words. The following passage contains two examples:

(24)   *Yet, by the theory developed here, the inertia of culture would exist because individuals and subgroups had influenced its direction and shape, **molding it**—even if imperceptibly across short time periods—to suit their particular needs, thereby incidentally **increasing the likelihood that subsequent individuals and subgroups could find ways to use it to their own advantages as well,** and could not alter it so greatly or rapidly.* (p. 69)

And, in a slightly different area, Quine's *Word and Object* averages 9 detached participles per 10,000 words. Here are two examples, to give the flavor of their function in his writing:

(25)   *There remain also other geometries, other in various ways. There are the more abstract ones, **culminating in topology,** which treat of the geometrical objects in decreasingly specific detail.* (p. 254)

(26)   *In steadfast laymanship they deplore them as departures from ordinary usage, **failing to appreciate that it is precisely by showing how to circumvent the problematic parts of ordinary usage that we show the problems to be purely verbal.*** (p. 261)

Tannahill's *Food in History* registers slightly higher at 14.7 detached participles per 10,000 words; this higher incidence is correlated with the fact that there are occasional depictive passages interspersed in the purely informative historical exposition. Examples (27) and (28) illustrate the use of detached participles in nondepictive and depictive passages, respectively:

(27)   *Of these seven magical oceans, **representing the staple needs of mankind in India** (other than grain), no less than three were of dairy products. Ghi was the essential cooking medium, although the poor had to make do with oil from sesamum or mustardseed, and the very poor with that of the safflower. Milk, though sometimes used fresh, was more often boiled until it reached a thick consistency, when it was used to make a gruel with whole grain or toasted barley meal.*   (pp. 159–160)

(28)   *The man of the house might first be offered an appetizer of one or two pieces of ginger and some salt. After this came boiled rice and bean soup and hot butter sauce, then cakes with ghi and fruit, and finally a piece of sugarcane to chew. If he were very poor, he would eat stale boiled rice with half-cooked gourds or other vegetables, or a grain porridge mixed with plenty of mustard stalk, **washing it down with an alkaline liquid which reputedly tasted like the water from a salt mine.***   (p. 163)

Nondepictive writing in the arts also appears to be low in detached participles. Read's style in *Henry Moore*, a study of the life and work of the great sculptor, is spare and highly nondepictive; even when descriptions of drawings and pieces of sculpture are presented, they do not evoke images, but rather refer to the illustrations. *Henry Moore* averages 11 detached participles per 10,000 words. Here is a representative paragraph, which contains one of the few detached participles:

(29)   *This supreme achievement is an upright form. Not content with this solution of the problem Moore decided to make a horizontal or 'reclining' version. First there is again a working model in bronze (Pl. 168) and then a final version which is 84 inches long (Pl. 169) The open forms in this reclining version are more complex and the internal form is more introverted and secretive. The over-all form is more organic and shell-like, and though the analogy of the human body is clearly intended, it is a natural formation of universal significance, **recalling the sculptor's early obsession for caves and eroded rocks.** 'Women', as Neumann says, 'has become the vessel absolute, the place of entrance and exit, a pure earth form made of cavities and hollows.'*   (p. 187)

Meyer's *Emotion and Meaning in Music*, a tightly reasoned discussion of music psychology and aesthetics, is very similar, with 12.8 detached participles per 10,000 words.[4] Examples (30) and (31) each contain a detached participle:

(30)   *The study of expectation which follows makes no pretense to completeness: first, because a complete and systematic study of the process of expectation would be a formidable task, **requiring a separate monograph of its own; second,** . . .* (p. 44)

(31)   *Thus it is that music, **mirroring the essential shape and substance of human experience,** from time to time contains sudden, shocking, clashes with unpredictable chance.* (p. 196)

What about literary criticism? I hypothesized that, as essentially nondepictive writing, it would be low in detached participles, but not as low as writing in the sciences, since some image evoking does occur. One cardinal example nicely supports this conjecture: Northrop Frye's study of William Blake, *Fearful Symmetry,* averages 18.9 detached participles per 10,000 words. To illustrate, I contrast a nondepictive passage containing a detached participle with two much more highly depictive passages exhibiting detached participles. Notice that each of two depictive passages begins with a reference to the "depiction" to follow — *his conception* in the first, and *the scene* in the second:

(32)   *Boehme is the first conspicuous example of the affinity between occult and left-wing inner-light Protestant traditions, **deriving as he did from the alchemic philosophers on the one hand and the Anabaptists on the other.*** (p. 153).

(33)   *It is particularly in his conception of the Creation and Fall that Boehme influenced Blake. This in Boehme occupies three stages, which Boehme calls "principles." The first "principle" is God conceived as wrath or fire, who torments himself inwardly until he splits open and becomes the second principle, God as love or light, **leaving behind his empty shell of pain,** which, because it is now God-forsaken, is abstract and dead.* (p. 153)

(34)   *. . . and the scene in which a prostitute shouts out a long apocalyptic interpretation of the Bible, **prophesying the immediate arrival of the Messianic kingdom,** Daniel's fifth monarchy, is in octave counterpoint to the same theme.* (p. 154)

Nondepictive writing, then, appears to be quite consistently low in frequency of detached participles, strongly supporting the claim that their

[4] This count ignores a few "speech-act absolutes," that is, those whose unexpressed subject is the "we" which includes the writer and the reader, as in:

(i)   ***Supposing that such automatic responses do exist,*** . . . , *it has not been definitely shown that they are differentiated as between types of affective experience.* (p. 17) distribution is heavily skewed in favor of depictive genres. The following table summarizes the findings for the nondepictive books I have discussed:

TEXT	DETACHED PARTICIPLES PER 10,000 WORDS
Pharmacology	5.0
Darwinism	8.5
Word and Object	9.0
Henry Moore	11.0
Music	12.8
Food in History	14.7
Fearful Symmetry	18.9

Comparing this table with the one given for the depictive books, we can see that whereas the nondepictive texts average fewer than 20 detached participles per 10,000 words, the depictive texts average more than 50.

Although the comparison between the depictive and nondepictive texts clearly reveals the skewing in the distribution of detached participles, it is only when we examine the detached participles themselves that we find the key to the explanation for this distribution. The detached participles that do occur in nondepictive writing share one interesting property: They tend to be stylistic alternates to other coordinate or subordinate clauses in a way in which the detached participles in depictive writing are not. As an illustration, consider one of the examples given from the pharmacology textbook:

(35)   *Even the pharmacist has very little to do with the preparation of drugs,* **most of them being manufactured by large companies.**
        (p. 1)

The detached participle in this example could very easily be replaced by a subordinate clause with *as,* with virtually no violation to the intended message:

(36)   *. . . as most of them are manufactured by large companies.*

Similarly, in the following example from *Darwinism and Human Affairs,* the detached participle is extremely close in expressive content to the nonrestrictive relative clause in (38):

(37)   *Preliminary findings already show that patterns of culture match predictions from the modern version of Darwinian theory to a much more significant degree than they were thought to in the past,* **indicating that objections from ontogenetic arguments must be reexamined.**   (p. 101)

(38)   . . . , *which indicates that objections from ontogenetic arguments*
        must be reexamined.

Strikingly enough, however, this type of paraphrasability is much less
characteristic of the detached participles in highly depictive passages. No
obvious paraphrase comes to mind for these three examples, for instance:

(39)   *She listened,* **marveling at the discernment in each name for the**
        complex illness of malaria, . . .   (*Madame Liang,* p. 114)
(40)   *The Indians stayed out of their way,* **leaving mute offerings of**
        food, deerskins, and feathered cloaks in the path of the ferocious
        invaders.   (*Explorers,* p. 36)
(41)   *Shopkeepers, dressed in white shirts and sarong-like skirts, with*
        embroidered skull-caps over their sharp Arabian faces, sat on
        string beds, outside their cavernous shops, **talking slowly and**
        smoking tall water-pipes.   (*Asia,* p. 13)

The unavailability of apt paraphrases for the detached participle in the
depictive texts is related, of course, to their very high frequency: There are
no other options at hand for conveying what they convey, and their functional load is thereby increased. But why are they difficult to paraphrase?
The answer, I suggest, lies precisely in the noncommittal relationship they
bear to the main clause, which makes them so well suited to scene depiction.
The point of depictive writing is to create scenes, and background material
in depictive discourse contributes to scene creation in an additive way,
temporal and logical relationships being essentially irrelevant. The point of
nondepictive writing, on the other hand, is to analyze situations, propose
and support claims, and enhance understanding by relating pieces of information. Background clauses there are called upon to participate in this
endeavor and must, to a much greater extent, bear explicitly labeled relationships with the main clause. As suggested earlier in the discussion of the
news article on South Africa, in nondepictive writing there is simply less
opportunity for the luxury of detached participles, whose relationship with
the main clause is so unspecified. Those that do occur are paraphrasable as
certain other types of clauses because the nondepictive context imposes
interpretations on them of precisely the logical and temporal relationships
explicitly expressed by those other types of clauses.

One incidental concomitant of this difference between the detached
participles actually found in depictive versus nondepictive writing is the
inordinate number of *being* clauses in the nondepictive texts. Example (35)
in an instance from *Pharmacology;* here are two more from other nondepictive texts:

(42)   *In one sense all behavior "has a genetic basis,"* **that sense being**
        that it also has an environmental basis.   (*Darwinism,* p. 100)

(43)   *Dryden and Pope translated epics and even dreamed of writing*
        *them, but never did, **the problems involved being insoluble on***
        ***their premises.** (Fearful symmetry, p. 165)*

Notice, again, the easy paraphrasability of these two examples with other
locutions; this appears always to be the case with detached participles
containing *being*. Of a total of 106 detached participles in the seven nondepictive books discussed here, no fewer than 11, or 10%, contain *being*. The
number of *being* clauses in the Erbaugh dissertation chapter is even higher:
Of the 66 detached participles, 10, or 15%, are *being* clauses, all of them
occurring in nondepictive portions. Here is one example:

(44)   *Kang Kang's family absolutely would not accept* (money), **the**
        situation being more problematic, *since Kang's mother was my*
        former teacher, . . .

These numbers contrast sharply with the situation in the depictive texts: Out
of a total of 246 detached participles surveyed from *Explorers, Asia, Madame Liang,* only one contained *being.*

   In this section I have examined the distribution of detached participles
among various types of written English and found a striking contrast
between depictive and nondepictive writing in the frequency with which
these clauses occur. I have claimed that the explanation for this contrast lies
in the suitability of the detached participle — given its indeterminate relationship with the main clause — for discourse whose purpose is to evoke
images, and its concomitant unsuitability for discourse whose background
information must be much more explicitly related to the figure material.

3. Grammatical Properties

   In Section 1, I pointed out that the detached participle provides "local"
background, that is, background for a particular other clause. This clause I
am referring to as the "main clause," although it may itself, of course, be
subordinate to yet another clause, as in (34) or in the following example in
which the detached participle is background to a relative clause:

(45)   *This pure pain is Satan or Lucifer, now cast off from God, who is*
        *also the inorganic matter of the created universe, **the created***
        ***universe being the third principle.** (Fearful Symmetry, p. 153)*

I suggested that this property of localness predicts essentially all of the
grammatical properties of the detached participle; showing that this is so is
the theme of this section.

Before I begin, however, a specification of the data base is in order. The data consist of 418 detached participles taken from the books and dissertation chapter discussed so far. The number of clauses from each source is given in the following table:

SOURCE	NUMBER OF CLAUSES
Madame Liang	87
Asia	85
Explorers	74
Erbaugh chapter	66
Fearful Symmetry	24
Food in History	22
Music	21
Word and Object	15
Darwinism	10
Pharmacology	8
Henry Moore	6
	418

My procedure was simply to begin at a random point in the work in question and list the properties for each detached participle encountered within the next *n* pages, where *n* was a random number greater than 20.

3.1. Tense and Subject

As pointed out by Fox (this volume), the dependence of the detached participle on the more prominent main clause with which it is associated allows it to be somewhat more "streamlined." That is, it can forego its own deictic tense marking and its own subject, since both of these are determinable from the main clause. This potential is always realized for tense; the participial form of the verb, which is the hallmark of the detached participle, is always tenseless.[5] In contrast, detached participles do sometimes have their own subjects. In the data, most of these independent subjects are in a part–whole relationship with the main clause subject:

(46)   *He looked so pitieous, **his little gray beard trembling on his chin**, that Madame Liang tried to comfort him.* (*Madame Liang,* p. 205)

---

[5] The "*having* verb*ed*" construction signals that the situation in the detached participle is prior to that in the main clause, but this is, of course, not deictic tense. Incidentally, the frequency of the *having* detached participle is very low: There were only eight instances in the data, only two of which were in the depictive texts.

(47)   *De Soto's personal belongings were also put up for auction, **his***
       five slaves and three horses fetching approximately two to three
       thousand cruzados each, . . .   (*Explorers*, p. 55)

Occasionally, the detached participle subject is coreferential with a main
clause nonsubject noun phrase, as in (48), or with no noun phrase at all in
the main clause, as in (49). As can be imagined by looking at these examples,
this type of detached participle subject occurs only in the nondepictive
writing in the data; even there it is rare.

(48)   *The varying potencies of members of a homologous series were*
       *explained by varying **affinities** of the drugs for the receptor,*
       affinity being the reciprocal of the dissociation constant (*1/KA*)
       of the drug–receptor combination.   (*Pharmacology*, p. 10)
(49)   *If the Augustan starts with a solitary prehuman God he is starting*
       with a cipher, and consequently will see in nature only a latent
       *harmony or "mathematic form," **reality becoming simpler and***
       more diagrammatic as it becomes clearer until it disappears into
       non-entity.   (*Fearful Symmetry*, p. 164)

Of the 418 clauses surveyed, only 57 — or 13.6% — had independent subjects. Because of its dependence on the main clause, then, the detached
participle never signals independent deictic tense and only rarely expresses
an independent subject.

3.2. Transitivity

In Hopper and Thompson (1980), it was shown that there is a high
correlation between the grounding function of a clause in discourse and its
transitivity, where transitivity can be seen as a composite of parameters
including not only whether a referential object is specified, but also such
parameters as kinesis, telicity, and punctuality. Clauses can then be ranked
according to the degree of transitivity they manifest. In general, clauses
performing backgrounding functions are low in transitivity: They often
have no object, and their predicates tend to be stative, atelic, and nonpunctual.

The fact that the detached participle provides background for the main
clauses predicts that instances of it should be very low in transitivity, as is all
background material. To test this prediction, I evaluated each clause in the
data for the following three key components of transitivity:

		High transitivity	*Low transitivity*
1.	Direct object:	specific	nonspecific or Ø
2.	Punctuality:	punctual	nonpunctual
3.	Aspect:	telic	atelic

If the features for low transitivity were distributed randomly across clauses in both figure and ground, then the numbers of detached participles with low transitivity and high transitivity features should be roughly equal. If, on the other hand, backgrounding correlates with low transitivity, then the majority of detached participles should exhibit features for low transitivity. That is, detached participles should tend to have nonspecific direct objects or to lack direct objects, and they should tend to have predicates that are nonpunctual and atelic. This prediction is strongly supported by the data.

Let us consider each of the three low transitivity features in turn.

3.2.1. Direct Object

Clauses were marked as having a specific object if the object was referential, either definite or indefinite, as in (50) and (51):

(50)   . . . , *searching **the country** for plunder* (*Explorers*, p. 45)
(51)   . . . , *examining with a magnifying glass **a tray of gold and silver coins*** (*Asia*, p. 37)

Any other object was considered to be nonspecific, such as those in (52) and (53):

(52)   . . . *complaining only **that the Japanese soldiers had found his secret grain storage a few days before*** (*Madame Liang*, p. 204)
(53)   . . . , *bringing **expectant ideo-motor sets** into play* (*Music*, p. 11)

An example of a clause with no object would be one like (54):

(54)   . . . , *riding with moderate comfort in their high Moorish saddles* (*Explorers*, p. 36)

The following table shows the direct object tallies. Note that although both clauses with no objects and clauses with nonspecific objects are low in transitivity, e.g., many languages treat them as equally intransitive in terms of morphosyntactic signals (see Hopper and Thompson, 1980), it seems reasonable to regard those with no objects as even lower than those with nonspecific objects.

		NUMBER	PERCENTAGE
High transitivity:	specific	120	30%
Low transitivity:	a. nonspecific	105 } 298	25% } 70%
	b. Ø	193	45%
Total		418	100%

In terms of type of direct object, 70% of the detached participles in the data are low in transitivity, the majority of those having no object at all.

3.2.2. Punctuality

Punctuality is a feature associated with the meanings of verbs and refers to the suddenness of an action, or the absence of a clear transitional phase between its onset and completion. Punctual verbs contrast with durative verbs, in which internal complexity is possible under normal interpretation, and with iterative verbs, which are also internally complex in the sense that there is repetition of identical punctual actions. A useful aid in determining whether a verb is punctual or not is to test its semantic compatibility with the phrase *for a long time.* In general, a verb is nonpunctual if it can be used in the frame:

(55)   Subject ___-ed *for a long time.*

and punctual otherwise. For example, in the detached participle in (56), the verb is nonpunctual, as (57) shows.

(56)   *Then, so she dreamed,* **gazing out** *over those unchanged palaces,* . . . *(Madame Liang,* p. 108)
(57)   *She* **gazed out** *over those unchanged palaces* **for a long time.**

The iterative verb in (58) is also nonpunctual, as suggested by (59).

(58)   *and by the time we got back to the hotel,* **sneezing** *and half blinded by the irritating sand particles,* . . . *(Asia,* p. 15)
(59)   *We* **sneezed** *for a long time.*

In contrast, (60) contains a punctual verb, since (61) is strange:

(60)   *Tuscaloosa managed to send runners to his war chiefs,* **summoning** *them to his capital at Mobila.* . . . *(Explorers,* p. 378)
(61)   **He summoned** *them to his capital* *for a long time.*

Of the 418 detached participles in the data, fully 372 of them, or 91%, are nonpunctual. Of these 372, 49, or 13%, are iterative, as in (58), and the rest are durative.

3.2.3. Aspect

The feature of aspect, unlike that of punctuality, is a feature of an entire predicate. A predicate that specifies an end point or conceptual boundary is said to be telic, whereas one that does not is atelic. The semantics of both the verb and its complements must be considered in determining whether a predicate is telic or not; for example, the predicates in (62b) and (63b) are telic, because an end point is specified, whereas their (a) counterparts are not:

(62) a. *She breathed quietly.*
      b. *She breathed in sharply.*
(63) a. *I drank tea.*
      b. *I drank up the tea.*

One clue to ascertaining the aspect of a predicate in English is the fact that only atelic predicates can be followed with a clause like the following:

(64) *. . . and then* subject *stopped ___-ing _____.*

For example, the telic predicate in the detached participle in (65) yields a contradiction in such a frame, as shown in (66).

(65) **Buckling on his armor,** *he was first into the fight and rallied his men.* (*Explorers*, p. 40)
(66) **He buckled on his armor, and then he stopped buckling on his armor.*

The atelic predicate in (67), on the other hand, is quite compatible with the added clause, as (68) shows:

(67) *They stood in front of us, **staring with hungry fascination.*** (*Asia*, p. 31)
(68) *They stared with hungry fascination, and then they **stopped staring with hungry fascination.***

Here are two more examples of telic detached participles in the data:

(69) *The old woman set a tray on a table, and **lifting the corner of her blue cotton jacket,** she wiped one eye and the other.* (*Madame Liang*, p. 129)
(70) *Diogenes Laertius mentions Druids as among the most ancient philosophers, **ranking them with Pythagoras and the Persian Magi.*** (*Fearful Symmetry*, p. 174)

Atelic predicates are often nonpunctual as well, but this is by no means a necessary concomitance. Example (71) shows a predicate that is iterative and therefore nonpunctual, but telic:

(71) *The crowded buses of the Afridi Transport careened past us up the road, **screaming to a halt whenever a group of baggy-trousered, rifle-bearing Pathans stood waiting,** . . .* (*Asia*, p. 40)

[62]

On the other hand, (72) exemplifies a predicate whose verb is semantically punctual, but which is atelic since, with a negative object, no end point is specified:

(72)   . . . *every line through A, B, and C that hits particles of both A and C passes between particles of B, **hitting none.** (Word and Object,* p. 256)

Of the 418 detached participles, 338, or 80%, of them were atelic.

The following table summarizes the percentage of detached participles bearing each of the low transitivity features we have examined.

FEATURE	%
Nonspecific object	70
Nonpunctual	91
Atelic	80

The transitivity properties of detached participles correlate very closely with those of backgrounded clauses in general and contrast sharply with those of foregrounded clauses. as independently distinguished in Hopper and Thompson (1980).[6] In the following table. the percentages for the three indexes of low transitivity are given for the set of backgrounded and foregrounded clauses analyzed in Hopper and Thompson (1980):

	CLAUSE	
FEATURE	BACKGROUNDED ($N = 85$)	FOREGROUNDED ($N = 47$)
Nonspecific object	82%	55%
Nonpunctual	90%	45%
Atelic	73%	12%

Comparing the two tables, we can see that detached participles are nearly identical with backgrounded clauses in general in the extent to which they show features of low transitivity. The "foregrounded" column in the latter table makes it clear that these properties are not characteristic of nonbackgrounded clauses.

[6] In Hopper and Thompson (1980). clauses from three narrative passages were analyzed as being either foregrounded or backgrounded according to functional criteria. spelled out there in detail. primarily involving the distinction between "main story line" and material that is subsidiary, motivational. evaluative. orientational. elaborative. etc.

Thus, the hypothesis that features of low transitivity are distributed in a highly skewed fashion in detached participles is strongly supported, and the correlation between backgrounding and low transitivity is reinforced.

4. Conclusion

I have attempted to characterize the discourse function of the detached participle in English and to show how its use as a local backgrounding device explains its distribution across discourse types as well as some of its grammatical properties. In so doing, I hope to have demonstrated the heavy reliance of grammar on the goals of the communicative event. That is, understanding grammar is inseparable from understanding the principles by which language users decide how to package an entire discourse.

Acknowledgments

I am grateful to Barbara Fox and Laurie Tuller for their help in collecting some of the data for this paper, and to the following people for valuable comments: Jack Du Bois, Barbara Fox, Paul Hopper, Jana Molhova, Paul Schachter, and R. McMillan Thompson. The responsibility for the use I have made of their advice rests entirely with me.

References

Berent, G. 1975. English absolutes in functional perspective. In *Papers from the parasession on functionalism*. Chicago: Chicago Linguistic Society.
Greenberg, J. 1966. Some universals of grammar with particular reference to the order of meaningful elements. In J. Greenberg (Ed.), *Universals of language*. Cambridge, Mass.: MIT Press.
Haiman, J. 1980. The iconicity of grammar. *Language* 56, 515–540.
Hopper, P., and Thompson, S. 1980. Transitivity in grammar and discourse. *Language* 56, 251–299.
Jespersen, O. 1933. *Essentials of English grammar*. London: Allen and Unwin.
Rappaport, G. 1979. Detachment and adverbial participle clauses in Russian. Unpublished doctoral dissertation, University of California, Los Angeles.

Sources of Data

Alexander, R. 1979. *Darwinism and human affairs.* Seattle: University of Washington Press.
Buck, P. S. 1969. *The three daughters of Madame Liang.* New York: John Day Co.

Carterette, E., and Jones, M. H. 1974. *Informal speech.* Berkeley and Los Angeles: University of California Press.

Chafe, W. (Ed.). 1980. *The Pear stories.* Norwood, N.J.: Ablex.

Erbaugh, Mary. 1982. Coming to order: natural selection and the origin of syntax in the Mandarin-speaking child. Unpublished doctoral dissertation. U.C. Berkeley.

Frye, N. 1947. *Fearful symmetry: a study of William Blake.* Princeton: Princeton University Press.

Goth, A. 1974. *Medical pharmacology: principles and concepts.* St. Louis: C. V. Mosby Co.

Meyer, L. B. 1956. *Emotion and meaning in music.* Chicago: University of Chicago Press.

Quine, W. V. O. 1960. *Word and object.* Cambridge, Mass.: MIT Press.

Read, H. 1967. *Henry Moore: a study of his life and work.* New York: Praeger.

Severin, T. 1967. *Explorers of the Mississippi.* London: Routledge and Kegan Paul.

Tannahill, R. 1974. *Food in history.* New York: Stein and Day.

Woodcock, G. 1966. *Asia, gods and cities.* London: Faber and Faber.

CHAPTER FOUR

Ergative, Passive, and Active in Malay Narrative

Paul J. Hopper

1. Introduction

There is often an assumption, in discussions of "discourse grammar," that discourse and sentence-level grammar constitute separate domains which may, ultimately, be shown to influence one another. If this is so, then we may proceed to study each of these levels independently; indeed, we may deny that discourse has any relevance for "syntax" defined as the formal aspects of sentences. Sentences may then be viewed simply as the "building blocks" of discourse, as Grimes and Glock suggest in their paper of 1970: "The 'chunks' [of information], which are sentences, have their own set of internal relationships; nothing here denies the validity of sentence grammar within its domain [p. 415]." Alternatively, discourse grammar is held to be a speculative agenda, to be postponed until the answers are in from syntax, as Morgan (1981) has suggested: "The burden is thus clearly on the discourse theorist to show that at least a fraction of these [syntactic] problems have explanations in discourse and/or functional terms. Frankly, I am skeptical that such explanations will ever be achieved [p. 144]." Morgan assumes that sentence-level structuralism represents a uniformly received body of knowledge, a "state of the art" which subsequent research must take as its point of departure:

> For example, how could such a [functionalist] theory explain cases of apparent functional disunity, like extraposed relatives, as in *the woman died in 70,000 B.C. who invented the wheel*, or verb-particle constructions like *John put the cat out*, to say

nothing of the numerous apparently purely formal conditions and constraints proposed by generative grammarians from Ross (1967) to Chomsky (1981)? [p. 144].

The present paper is not intended as a polemic against ideas such as these; yet Morgan's very examples cry out for discussion along functionalist lines. The first sentence (*The woman died in 70,000 B.C. who invented the wheel*) sounds utterly bizarre to me; I cannot place it into any context, no matter how hard I try, and it thus seems to be an example of a sentence that a correct theory ought NOT to account for.[1] As to the second example, involving the well-known verb–particle construction, the discourse explanation seems rather obvious: with some modifications, the particle appears to the right of the object precisely when the object is anaphoric, that is, is either a pronoun or a previously mentioned noun. At the sentence level this distribution is hard to state, as the structural description of the rule has to make reference to (*a*) pronouns [obligatory], and (*b*) nouns [optional]. THE AFFECTED NPs CAN ONLY BE CAPTURED AS A CLASS BY REFERENCE TO DISCOURSE. It is ironic that the very two examples that Morgan presents to show the impossibility of discourse grammar illustrate nicely the very reasons why sentence-level syntax will not work: (*a*) it is forced to claim grammaticality for sequences which no amount of introspection can provide a setting for; and (*b*) it provides the WRONG explanation for the grammaticality of quite ordinary sequences.

In this paper I discuss some central constructions in a variety of Written Malay with a view, implicitly, to demonstrating that no approach to grammar (morphology and syntax) that separates LOCAL (more or less: clause level) from GLOBAL (more or less: discourse level) factors can work. I thus reject all approaches that insist on the autonomy of the "sentence," both the building blocks approach of Grimes and others, and the generative-transformationalist approach of much current work on syntax.

A consequence of the decision to work with discourse material is the assumption that data from "intuition," and indeed any data which were presented for the purposes of linguistic analysis, are suspect. An ideal corpus

[1] And, indeed, Morgan's "sentence" is ungrammatical precisely because it shows functional disunity, that is, a lack of concord between its form (extraposed relative) and the function which this form must have. I take this function to be something like discourse salience of the relative clause and low focus on the predicate. In Morgan's "sentence" we have no way of evaluating the relative salience of the main clause predicate vis-à-vis the relative clause without a context, and we can only find it odd that the date of this person's death overrides in significance the information that the inventor of the wheel was a woman. The whole example is thoroughly misbegotten, and emphasizes the methodological importance of working with natural rather than fake data. In an essay of Quiller-Couch's I find the following example of an extraposed relative: "In literature as in life he makes himself felt who not only calls a spade a spade but has the pluck to double spades and redouble." Here the lame main-clause predicate *makes himself felt* would be incongruous in the salient position at the end of the sentence, and the main point of the sentence is in the relative clause itself; hence the extraposition.

is one which is extensive enough to provide numerous examples of the construction being studied together with ample discourse contexts for each example.

My corpus for this paper will be the Malay autobiography of Abdullah 'Munshi' (ᶜAbd Allāh ibn ᶜAbd al-Qadir, Munshi), known as the *Hikayat Abdullah*. Abdullah Munshi was born in Malacca in 1795, and died on the Hajj in 1855, probably in Mecca. The language of the autobiography is perhaps best characterized as "early modern" Malay, having affiliations with both modern Standard Malay and the antecedent classical language of the traditional Hikayat ('histories'). In regard to the constructions being discussed here, there are slight differences between Abdullah's usage and modern usage. I therefore regard the corpus as a unitary idiolect describable in its own terms and having linguistic interest as a self-contained variety of Malay. Abdullah was a native speaker of Malay (there is ample evidence in the autobiography and in the accounts of his contemporaries for this fact); thus my use of the term "idiolect" should not be viewed as equivalent to "idiosyncratic."

2. Passive and Ergative: An Outline

2.1. The Malay "Passive"

The two constructions that form the core of this paper share a common morphology usually called "passive." This morphology is best presented as having one form for first and second person pronoun agents, and another form for third person agents.

With first person pronoun agents, the stem of the verb is prefixed with the proclitic form of the pronoun *aku* 'I', namely *ku-:*

sa-telah satu muka kitab itu **ku-**   *bacha*
after   one page book the 1AGT read
'after I had read one page of the book' (44)[2]

The gloss 1AGT is to be interpreted as first person proclitic agent of the passive.

With third person agents, the prefix *di-* appears on the verb, and the agent, if a pronoun, is enclitic to the prefixed verbal stem in the form *-nya:*

maka **di-** buboh- **nya-** lah   tanda-tangan- nya
then PASS fix   3AGT LAH signature   his
'then he affixed his signature' (27)

---

[2] References are to the Malay Literature Series edition of the *Hikayat Abdullah*, in two volumes (Abdullah 1932), paged continuously.

The gloss PASS refers to the passive prefix for third person agents, and 3AGT glosses the agentive pronoun -*nya*. The gloss LAH is used for a discourse particle which will be discussed later. With noun agents an agentive phrase similar to the English *by*-phrase is added:

ada   pun aku di- jualkan **oleh ibu-** **ku** ka-pada enam
happen PUN I   PASS sell   by mother my to   six
tujoh orang
seven person
'So it happened that I was sold by my mother to six or seven people (12)

(a reference to symbolic adoption). Occasionally the preposition *oleh* is omitted. The agent may also be absent, in which case the passive is signaled solely by the verbal prefix *di-*:

tiada ia **di-**   *lepaskan*
not he PASS   set-free
'he is not set free' (19)

    The patient of the passive construction is either unmarked or is signaled by the "accusative" preposition *akan*:

Hata maka sa-telah sudah di-   dengar oleh Tuan Raffles **akan**
now then after   already PASS hear by Mr.   ACC
perkataan dalam surat itu . . .
words   in   letter that
'Now when Mr. Raffles had heard the words in that letter . . . ' (85)

This accusative preposition is not found when the patient precedes the verb. The preposition is in complementary distribution with the verbal suffix -*kan*, however, and with this suffix the patient may be pre- or postposed. The suffix -*kan* has a number of local functions in Malay, including causative and "instrumental" (denoting that the patient of the verb is the instrument with which the action is carried out); the general function appears to be that of "transitivization," as discussed in Hopper and Thompson (1980:260–261).

2.2. *The Two Constructions Passive and Ergative*

    The existence of two distinct structural types associated with passive morphology in Malay has been noted by Chung (1975) and Cartier (1979) in their discussions of Modern Indonesian (Bahasa Indonesia). In this paper I do not undertake to compare Abdullah's usage with that of Bahasa Indonesia beyond noting that in earlier Malay the structural difference between the two passives appears less rigid, and that there is some overlap between the two constructions in discourse. This overlap suggests, of course, that the "grammatical" difference between the two constructions is derivative of their discourse contexts. Like Cartier (1979), I regard one of the constructions as ergative and the other as passive. In the discussion which follows the passive is distinguished from the ergative on both grammatical and discourse-functional grounds. I later show that it is the discourse-functional difference which is primary, and that the grammatical difference should be seen as derivative of the discourse function. Cartier (1979) similarly argues for the distinction of passive and ergative in both grammar and discourse, but does not assign priority to one distinction over the other.

Fundamentally the passive is distinguished from the ergative in two ways:

1. The patient NP precedes the verb:
   maka dua puncha kiri kanan itu di-   matikan
   then two ends   left right   the PASS knot
   'and the two ends to the right and left are knotted'   (18)

2. The discourse role of the passive is a BACKGROUNDING one. It tends to denote states, customary actions, descriptions, and the like, and is used less often to denote actions which happen once or which provide a story line. In some of these respects the Malay passive resembles the English passive, for example, in its frequent use to describe artifacts. Some examples of the discourse functions of the Malay passive are as follows:

(*a*) Customary or habitual actions
   karna demikian- lah di-   perbuat oleh orang tua-tua
   because thus   LAH PASS do   by   person old:PLUR
   'for this is the way the old people do it'   (11)

(*b*) Resultant state
   ada   pun sakalian baris itu di-   atur-   nya   tiga-tiga lapis
   happen PUN every   rank the PASS draw-up 3AGT three   fold
   'It happened that they had drawn up all the ranks in three rows.'   (77)

(*c*) Indefinite agent
   dan tiada pula engkau di-   hinakan orang
   and not also you   PASS scorn   person
   'Moreover, people will not scorn you.'   (17)

(*d*) Descriptions
   ada pun apit China itu di-   perbuat dari-pada rotan sega
   it-is PUN press Chinese the PASS make   out-of   rattan fine
   'Now the Chinese press was made out of the finest rattan . . .'   (18)

Like the English passive, and unlike the passive in certain other languages, the Malay passive occurs freely with and without an agent.

The construction named ergative is formally similar to the passive. The prime distinguishing feature of the ergative is that the patient NP follows the

[71]

verb, whereas in the passive the patient always precedes. Frequently the patient NP of the ergative is preceded by the accusative preposition *akan.*

In its discourse function the ergative serves to FOREGROUND events (cf. Hopper, 1979c). It has a predilection for individuated actions, generally of a concrete, visible kind (Cartier, 1979:181), and usually sequenced (Hopper, 1979c). Thus passages like the following abound in the corpus:

Ada   pun api- nya itu datang dari sebab orang kapal itu minum
happen PUN fire the that came from reason men ship the smoke
cherutu di-   champakkan- nya   puntong cherutu itu ka-dalam kapal
cheroot PASS throw-away   3AGT stub   cheroot the into   ship
maka menjangkit- lah   ka-pada tali-tali itu, maka di-   makan-
and spread   LAH into   ropes the and   PASS consume
nya- lah   kapal itu
3AGT LAH ship   the
'Now the fire came about because the crewmen were smoking cheroots, and they threw away the stubs into the boat, and the fire spread to the ropes and burned up the ship.' (91)

The ergative foregrounds "transitive" events. Intransitive events, such as *menjangkit* 'spread to' in the passage cited, are foregrounded by attaching the discourse particle *-lah* to the verb. This particle may also be added to the ergative verb—but not to the passive verb—if the narrated event is of special importance.

2.2.1. The Ergative with Preverbal Patient

We have seen that the canonical word order for the ergative is Verb–Agent–Patient. The patient is thus placed after the verb, and it is this positional characteristic which basically distinguishes the ergative from the passive. Yet ergative patients may also precede the verb. Almost always when this happens the particle *pun* follows the patient. Another strategy for preposing patients is to quantify the NP with *semua-nya* 'all of them'; this quantifier is then "floated" to the right of the patient, so that it immediately precedes the verb. Both strategies are examplified in the following passage:

Maka segala pengana itu pun di-   bahagikan- lah   ka-pada segala
and all   cakes   the PUN PASS distribute LAH to   all
budak-budak, dan wang- nya di-   ambil oleh guru- nya itu, dan
boy:PLUR   and money the PASS take by   teacher the that and
bunga chandana   semua-nya di- bahagikan.
flower sandalwood all-of-them PASS distribute
'Then all the cakes were passed around to all the boys, and the money

was taken by the teacher, and the sandalwood blossoms were all passed around.' (20)

Here both *pun* and *semua-nya* are used to front the patient NP before the ergative verb. It will be noticed, however, that the second ergative clause in the passage, *dan wang-nya di-ambil oleh guru-nya itu* 'and the money was taken by the teacher', is not distinguishable from the passive. Indeed, it is only because it is part of an event sequence (i.e., a semantic criterion) that we are entitled to refer to this clause as ergative. Such clauses are rare, but they do occur, especially when the patient is highly topical and anaphoric. Another example is the following:

maka **duit** *itu di-* **ambil** *oleh ibu-bapa- nya, di- belikan- nya*
then money the PASS take by parents his PASS use-to-buy 3AGT
penganan atau barang-barang makanan, di- makan- nya
cakes or things eating PASS eat 3AGT
'Then his parents take the money and use it to buy cakes or other things to eat, and they eat them.' (12)

(can -nya refer to plural referent ?)

In the first clause the patient *duit itu* 'the money (just mentioned)' precedes the verb without *pun* or a floated quantifier. Again, the clause is formally indistinguishable from a passive.

The point is that although there is a very high correlation between ergative and VSO word order on the one hand and passive and OVS word order on the other, the correlation is not absolute. Evidently the VSO word order itself is not a grammaticalized signal of foregrounding, but is rather a reflex of something else. I return to this at the end of the paper, where I suggest that the VSO word order is simply a strategy for focusing the verb.

3. Transitivity

Is there some less subjective and intuitive means by which the semantic difference between ergative and passive clauses can be characterized?

I have referred to the fact that both passive and ergative clauses are transitive in the sense that the action signaled by them includes reference to a patient and, usually, an agent. In this section I will examine this premise in detail, making use of the Transitivity Theory elaborated by myself and Sandra Thompson (Hopper and Thompson, 1980).

3.1. The Transitivity Theory

In the work referred to, Transitivity is viewed not as a simple matter of the number of participant NPs, but as a discourse-derived relationship which is stronger in proportion to the intensity of the event which the clause is reporting. The intensity — that is, THE DEGREE OF TRANSITIVITY — of the event is measured as an aggregate of a number of parameters, each of which contributes in some way to the transitivity relationship. The parameters are, it should be emphasized, discourse parameters; yet either alone or in combination they can be shown to have consistent typological effects on the morphosyntax of the clause. The article cited documents in detail these local effects. The parameters are the following:

A. *Participants:* A clause with both an agent and a patient is more Transitive than a clause with only one of these.
B. *Aspect:* A clause containing a telic (point-oriented) predicate is more Transitive than a clause whose predicate is atelic.
C. *Kinesis:* Clauses which signal an action of some kind, involving movement in either patient or agent, are more Transitive than those in which no action is signaled.
D. *Affectedness of patient:* A clause containing a patient which is physically affected by the action of the verb is more transitive than one whose patient is not affected.
E. *Polarity:* Affirmative clauses are more Transitive than negative clauses.
F. *Modality:* Clauses containing a realis predicate (i.e., a predicate which reports a real occurrence) are more Transitive than those in an irrealis mood such as subjunctive.
G. *Potency of agent:* A clause whose agent is human or animate is more Transitive than one whose agent is inanimate or incapable of spontaneous action.
H. *Individuation of patient:* Clauses whose patients are definite/referential are more Transitive than clauses whose patients are indefinite/nonreferential.
I. *Volitionality:* A clause whose action is carried out deliberately by the agent is more transitive than one whose agent is acting without intention.
J. *Punctuality:* A clause whose predicate occurs without a perceptible transition between onset and conclusion is more Transitive than one whose predicate has discernible duration.

These parameters help define Transitive clauses which typically have morphosyntactic properties of Transitivity and which function in discourse to carry the more salient, foregrounded, actions. It should therefore be the case that in Malay the ergative clause will typically have a higher index for the Transitivity parameters than the passive clause. Fifty clauses of each type were taken from random pages of the corpus; on each page selected, every clause of each type was included in the sample. In addition, 50 clauses of a third clause type, the *meng-* active (a construction not yet discussed), were also examined for the same purpose.

3.2. Criteria for Applying the Parameters

The criteria that were used to compare the clauses were objective ones so far as this was possible. Wherever possible, a concrete morphemic or syntactic construction was used as the criterion, or an obvious semantic feature like 'human'. Occasionally, this meant that the Transitivity parameter in question had to be extended or restricted somewhat. For the purposes of the present study, the following criteria were among those adopted:

1. Parameter (D), affectedness of patient, was defined as plus if the patient NP was preceded by the preposition *akan,* or if the verb contained the suffix *-kan.* The meanings of *-kan/akan* are compatible with 'affected patient' but not entirely commensurate with it.
2. With regard to Parameter (H), patients were considered to be definite if they consisted of a proper name, a personal pronoun, or a noun restricted by one of the definite articles or other definite modifiers (demonstratives, possessives, etc.).
3. With regard to Parameter (G), agents were considered to be potent that is, capable of spontaneous action, if they were human, and not otherwise.

These restrictions slightly bias the conclusions away from the high end of the transitivity continuum, and thus conservatively reduce the degree of difference between ergative and passive clauses. For example, the parameter of patient individuation (H) should be plus if the patient is indefinite, provided it is referential; but the parameter as defined here allows only for definite/referential patients to be individuated.

The criterion used for determining whether a clause was ergative or passive was a simple one involving word order. Basically, clauses with verb-initial word order were treated as ergative, and clauses with patient-initial word order were treated as passive. We have noted that this distinction occasionally fails, in that semantically ergative clauses may have an initial patient. If the patient was marked with *pun* or a rightward floated quantifier, the clause was counted as ergative. The effect of marking an NP with *pun* or a quantifier to the right is to dislocate the NP from the rest of the clause, thus effectively allowing the clause to begin with the verb. This dislocation derives in turn from the "lookback" distance between the referent of the NP in question and its previous reference in the discourse; the relationship between such phenomena involving anaphoric "continuity" (Givón, 1983)

[75]

and ergative case-marking in Malay deserves further research. Clauses in which the patient preceded the verb without an overt topicalizer like *pun* or a quantifier were rigidly counted as passive. Again, this procedure intro- duces a slight bias in favor of the passive, in other words, a bias which tends to narrow slightly the difference between ergative and passive. The objective of such adjustments was to ensure that subjective assignment of values was kept to a minimum, and that where they were necessary they should not result in exaggerated claims but if anything in understatements.

3.3. Transitivity Index of a Sample Clause

As an illustration of how the Transitivity index of each of the 150 clauses examined was calculated, we will take the following clause:

karna   binatang itu di-   laparkan beberapa hari
because animals the PASS starve   several   day
'because the animals had been starved for several days'   (51)

This clause qualifies as a passive one, since the patient immediately precedes the passive verb. The Transitivity index of this clause was 5, since out of a possible 10 points for the Transitivity parameters it scored as follows:

A. *Participants:* 0
   The clause contains a patient (*binatang itu*), but no expressed agent.
B. *Aspect:* 0
   The action of the verb is atelic, since the act *laparkan* 'starve, keep hungry' is not point-oriented.
C. *Kinesis:* 0
   No action or motion is predicated by the verb.
D. *Affectedness of patient:* 1
   The verb has the suffix *-kan*, therefore the patient is considered to be affected.
E. *Polarity:* 1
   The clause is affirmative, and is therefore plus for this parameter.
F. *Modality:* 1
   The clause is realis ("indicative").
G. *Potency of agent:* 0
   No agent being specified, the clause cannot be marked plus for this feature.
H. *Individuation of patient:* 1
   The patient NP *binatang itu* includes the article/demonstrative *itu*.
I. *Volitionality:* 1
   The context makes it clear that the act of depriving the animals (elephants) of food was done intentionally in order to weaken them.

J. *Punctuality:* 0
The event continued over an extended period of time (*beberapa hari,* 'several days').

For the most part there was little difficulty in assigning the values of the parameters to a given clause. In the clause discussed here, the values are nearly all objective — some through overt morphosyntactic markers (e.g., D, H), some through unambiguous semantic features (C, F), and some through context. The volitionality of the act, for example, is determined by the facts of the narrative: One of the strategies involved in capturing a wild elephant is to trap it and deprive it of food for a while in order to weaken it.

4. Analysis of Discourse Functions of Major Clause Types

The transitivity index of each of the 150 clauses in the sample was, calculated in this way, and averages for each type were obtained. For passive and ergative clauses the averages for the 50-clause sample of each type were:

Passive: 4.78
Ergative: 8.62

The ergative clause thus emerges as significantly more Transitive in the composite sense than the passive clause. This local (i.e., semantic and morphosyntactic) difference corresponds to the global (discourse) functional difference between the two. Typologically, the Transitivity parameters are significant at both of the levels referred to here as "local" and "global":

1. They define at the local level the assignment of case and aspect morphosyntax.
2. They converge at points of the discourse where highlighting of the action and advancement of the story line occur.

But in different languages, and in different constructions in the same language, these parameters interact in different ways, so that some may make a more important contribution than others. The data concerning the passive and ergative in Malay suggest that OVERALL the ergative construction is considerably higher in transitivity than the passive. But this overall figure does not necessarily mean that the difference is equal for each parameter, nor that the ergative is higher than the passive in each parameter (although this might happen to be the case). It is therefore interesting to compare the ergative and the passive scores parameter by parameter.

[77]

TABLE 1

Percentages of Passive and Ergative Clauses with Plus for Each of the Transitivity Parameters

PARAMETER	PASSIVE	ERGATIVE	
A. Participants	68	90	
B. Aspect	48	88	
C. Affected patient	40	64	*! surprising*
D. Kinesis	42	84	
E. Polarity	90	98	
F. Modality	82	90	
G. Agent potency	48	88	*not surprising*
H. Patient individuation	84	94	
I. Volitionality	60	88	
J. Punctuality *backgroundity*	28	70	

Table 1 shows for the 50 passive and 50 ergative clauses in the sample the percentage of clauses marked as plus for each of the parameters. Of the 10 parameters, 4 (aspect, kinesis, potency of agent, and punctuality) show a difference of 40 percentage points or more between ergative and passive. For the other 6 the difference is less than 30 percentage points. In descending order of differential, the parameters are thus ranked as in Table 2:

TABLE 2

Ranking of Differentials between Ergative and Passive Clauses for Each Transitivity Parameter

RANK	PARAMETER	% PLUS IN ERGATIVE	% PLUS IN PASSIVE	DIFFERENCE
1 =	Kinesis	84	42	42
1 =	Punctuality	70	28	42
3 =	Aspect	88	48	40
3 =	Agent potency	88	48	40
5	Volitionality	88	60	28
6	Affected patient	64	40	24
7	Participants	90	68	22
8	Patient individuation	94	84	10
9 =	Polarity	98	90	8
9 =	Modality	90	82	8

The prominent difference between the two clause types in the first four of the ranked parameters in Table 2 points strongly to a different discourse role for the ergative as opposed to the passive. The parameters that are most distinctive for the ergative are precisely those which typically make the most contribution to the event line of the narrative. They suggest human actors

[78]

carrying out rapid, sequenced actions. These are the components which convey the essence of a narrative discourse.

A further important consideration is the absolute percentage of plus parameters for each clause type. Thus it can be seen that punctuality, which strongly differentiates ergative from passive, is nonetheless a low-ranking feature of the ergative, ranking ninth among the 10 parameters. Patient individuation, on the other hand, which constitutes a weak differentiator of passive and ergative, can be seen to be present in a high percentage of both clause types (84% for passive, 94% for ergative). The observation with regard to punctuality means simply that significant events are likely to be, but do not have to be, punctual. But the high counts for definiteness of patient in both ergative and passive call for a more detailed explanation. For although in general in narrative discourse we may expect to find a fairly high proportion of definite/referential NPs, these tend to be distributed in the discourse in such a way that event-centered, "foregrounded" parts of the narrative have significantly more than the slower, "backgrounded" parts (Hopper and Thompson, 1980:287–292). In order to explain the high figures for definite/referential patients in both ergative and passive, and the low value for the differential between the two, I turn now to a third major clause type, the active.

4.1. The Active

The active is characterized by the prefix *meng-* on the verb (with some simple phonological changes); a small group of verbs, including *pergi* 'go' and *makan* 'eat', do not take the prefix. The word order is typically Agent–Verb–Patient.

The active is often used in discourse to suggest a slowed tempo of narrative, and is thus usual in backgrounded detail when scenic or characterological description is being given. It may also be used for events, especially introductory events in an episode. It is therefore often found in alternation with ergative and the event-making clitic *-lah*, as in the following:

sa-bermula maka ada-   lah   kira-kira enam tujuh belas bulan
now   and   happen LAH about   six   seven teen months
lama- nya maka Tuan Thomsen pun   datang- lah   pula ka- Malaka. Ia
time   its then Mr.   PUN came   LAH again to Malacca he
mengatakan isteri- nya itu sudah   mati di- laut, ada kira-kira
MENG say wife his the ASPECT die   at sea was about
empat lima hari akan   sampai ka- negeri England.
four   five days before arrive in   country
'And now it came about that after sixteen or seventeen months Mr.

[79]

Thomsen came back to Malacca. He said that his wife had died at sea, some four or five days before reaching England.' (125)

In a very typical use of the active, we find foregrounded clauses like *datang-lah* 'came' alternating with the *meng-* verb *mengatakan* 'say, tell' (stem form *katakan*), in which the action is an interpolation. The *meng-* verb is frequently found in positions which would be identified in some other languages as subordinate clauses, for example:

merika'itu berkirim surat ka- Benggala meminta   tolong
they   send   letter to Bengal   MENG ask help
'They sent a letter to Calcutta asking assistance.' (137)

The distinction "main clause – subordinate clause" is not easy to make in Malay. There appear to be no cogent reasons for distinguishing them from full sentences on the one hand or (as here) the second verb in a clause having two verbs. The appropriate way of looking at *meng-* clauses in such contexts is to view them as sharing a global function of 'backgrounding', of which 'subordination' is merely one manifestation.

It should be added here that the triple contrast passive – ergative – active does not exhaust the complexities of Malay discourse. Further variously affixed verb forms occur as well, and also the bare unaffixed stem of the verb. The account given in the present study thus falls short of a complete analysis. Yet the three clause types account for a major part of the corpus, and the data given and discussed here point to consistent conclusions.

4.2. *Transitivity and the* Meng- *Active*

The Transitivity counts for clauses whose verb has the prefix *meng-* is consistent with the hypothesized backgrounding function of the construction. The average count for 50 clauses on randomly chosen pages of the corpus is given in Table 3, which compares the figure obtained with the figures for passive and ergative clauses. The figure for the *meng-* active, it can be seen, is very close to that of the passive. It contrasts with the figure for ergative clauses, and suggests that in terms of global function the active is grouped with the passive.

TABLE 3
*Average Transitivity Count for 50-clause Sample
of Each Major Clause Type*

	PASSIVE	ERGATIVE	ACTIVE (*meng-*)
Average transitivity count	4.78	8.62	5.26

[80]

TABLE 4
Percentages of Passive, Ergative, and Active Clauses
with Plus for Each of the Transitivity Parameters

PARAMETER	PASSIVE	ERGATIVE	ACTIVE (*meng-*)
A. Participants	68	90	74
B. Aspect	48	88	50
C. Affected patient	40	64	28
D. Kinesis	42	84	26
E. Polarity	90	98	98
F. Modality	82	90	38
G. Agent potency	48	88	90
H. Patient individuation	84	94	22
I. Volitionality	60	88	62
J. Punctuality	28	70	24

In a previous section we compared the differences between clause types for each of the Transitivity parameters, noting which parameters are most strongly marked as differentiators between the two constructions. The same procedure may now be applied to the active, comparing it with both of the other two clause types. Table 4 gives the percentage of plus scores for each parameter for the 50-clause sample, and displays this information beside the information already given in Table 1, and Table 5 gives the ranking for the 10 parameters in the case of active clauses. Finally, Table 6 gives the differential scores for the three pairs: passive – active; ergative – active; and ergative – passive. The members of each pair are ordered as in the table title; therefore, in cases where the second member of the pair outranks the first, the score is displayed with a minus sign in front of it. Thus, a score of – 6 for

TABLE 5
Ranking of Transitivity Parameters in Sample
of 50 Clauses Containing Meng- *Active*

RANK	PARAMETER	PERCENTAGE PLUS
1	Polarity	98
2	Agent potency	90
3	Participants	74
4	Volitionality	62
5	Aspect	50
6	Modality	38
7	Affected patient	28
8	Kinesis	26
9	Punctuality	24
10	Patient Individuation	22

[81]

TABLE 6
Differential Scores for Transitivity Parameters between Passive–Active, Ergative–Active, and Ergative–Passive[a]

	PARAMETER	PASSIVE–ACTIVE	ERGATIVE–ACTIVE	ERGATIVE–PASSIVE
A.	Participants	−6	16	22
B.	Aspect	−2	38	40
C.	Affected patient	12	36	24
D.	Kinesis	16	58	42
E.	Polarity	−8	0	8
F.	Modality	45	52	8
G.	Agent potency	−42	−2	40
H.	Patient individuation	62	72	10
I.	Volitionality	−2	26	28
J.	Punctuality	4	46	42

[a] The numbers are obtained from Table 4 by subtracting the second member of the pair from the first; a minus figure indicates that the figure for the second member was higher than the figure for the first member of the pair.

the participants parameter in the Passive–Active column means that 6% more active clauses than passive clauses had two participants.

4.3. Discussion

The figures presented in Tables 4–6 point to some significant facts about the distribution of labor among the three major clauses types. Considering Table 6, which shows the differences between each pair of clause types in the percentage of transitivity parameters marked plus in the samples, we may note that a small number means that the members of the pair are functionally similar, whereas a large number suggests that that parameter is a significant selector for the clause type(s) in question. Thus we note that the parameter of polarity—the affirmative or negative value of a clause—is virtually irrelevant to differentiating clause types. On the other hand, kinesis significantly distinguishes the ergative from the active (58% difference) and from the passive (42% difference), although it does not distinguish active from passive (16% difference).

The active is most sharply distinguished from the passive and the ergative in the two parameters modality (45% and 52%) and patient individuation (62% and 72%). For each of these scores we can see from Table 4 that the *meng-* active is the lower in transitivity in each pair passive–active and ergative–active. The low score in the modality parameter can be explained from the fact that the *meng-* prefix, because of its backgrounding function, is very frequently found on complement and other dependent verbs.

[82]

The high differentiation of the active in the scores for patient individuation (i.e., definiteness of patient) suggests an answer to the question posed earlier concerning the unexpectedly low differentiation between the ergative and the passive in this parameter. Definiteness of patient is clearly an important selector for both passive and ergative. Conversely, we might expect that nonindividuated patients would tend to be found with *meng-* active verbs. This is in fact repeatedly the case, for example:

maka masing-masing memegang   pedang
and   each-one   MENG draw sword
'then each of them drew his sword'   (134)
maka ia memberi   hormat
then   he MENG give honor
'then he paid his respects'   (138)
maka hari itu juga ia memberi   wakil   ka-pada Kapitan Da'ud
and   day that also he MENG give command to   Captain
'And that day also he handed over command to Captain Da'ud.'   (137)

In all of these, and many other, examples of *meng-* active clauses the patient is not modified by a determiner, and is therefore considered nonindividuated. The patient in such cases is a generic or cognate object which does not REFER to a specific member of its semantic class. It should be emphasized that *meng-* on the verb does not signal or code the presence of an indefinite agent. If this were so, the phenomenon would be explicable at the local level through straightforward semantic interpretation of the morphosyntactic construction. What happens is more subtle: A "conspiracy" of discourse factors, of which the degree of referentiality of the participants is among the most important, results in a certain arrangement of the elements of the clause, accompanied by certain morphosyntactic side effects. Ignoring for the moment the strictly morphological side effects (affixation and cliticization), and considering only the word order of the main elements, verb, agent, and patient, we find that each of the three construction types selects one of these elements for clause-initial position.

1. The ERGATIVE selects the verb. Exceptions to this rule are the following: (*a*) NPs that are marked as revived topics by the enclitic particle *pun* or by a right-floated quantifier such as *semua-nya* 'all of them', and (*b*) the proclitic first person agent *ku-*, which is morphologically bound to the prefix position. In the case of the NP-*pun* construction and the type in which a referent is first mentioned and then taken up with *semua-nya,* as in:

dan bunga chandana   semua-nya di-bahagikan
and flower sandalwood all-of-them be-distributed
'and the sandalwood blossoms were all passed around'   (20)

it can be seen that the effect of the quantifier and of *pun* is to ISOLATE THE REVIVED TOPIC FROM THE VERB, so that the clause is effectively verb initial. A right-floated quantifier can isolate the topic NP in this way because it is a highly continuous element; its referent has in fact just been mentioned (i.e., *bunga chandana* 'sandalwood blossoms'). The "oldness" of the quantifier thus neutralizes the "newness" of the NP and permits it to be treated as detached from the clause as a whole.

2. The ACTIVE with *meng-* is, to put it imprecisely, an agent-oriented construction. It permits the agent NP (full noun or independent pronoun) to precede the verb.

3. Finally, the PASSIVE, which shares the morphology of the ergative, is "patient oriented," and permits the patient NP to precede the verb.

These three position characteristics correspond exactly to the discourse functions that they perform, as shown by the Transitivity features that are most prominently associated with them and by the more general features of their discourse contexts.

1. The initial verb—that is, the ergative—narrates sequenced events which pertain to the main line of the discourse. It is NONPREDICATIONAL, in the sense that neither of the participant NPs constitutes a starting point for the clause; the clause does not "say something about" one of the NPs, but instead focuses purely on the event—the change—itself. The ergative scores high on all the transitivity parameters, but especially on the ones most characteristic of events: telicity (goal directedness), agency, kinesis (change), and punctuality (quickness).

2. The initial patient—that is, the passive—is a PREDICATIONAL clause type with topic–comment structure. Its starting point is the patient NP, and the nature of the agent is relatively unimportant to the intention of the clause. The passive "says something about" the patient. The passive thus scores low on all the parameters involving the agent—number of participants, agent potency, and volitionality—and scores high on the parameter of patient individuation.

3. The initial agent—that is, the active—is also a predicational clause type. Its topic is the agent, and its patient is often less relevant to the context. The active "says something about" the agent. It is therefore high in the agent parameter of agent potency, and low in the patient parameters of patient affectedness, patient individuation, and number of participants. The active is also low in volitionality, perhaps because of its affinity, which it shares with the passive, for nonevent, backgrounded contexts.

The obvious mirror image relationship between the active and the passive suggests, as Talmy Givón has pointed out to me, that the active should be considered an antipassive. In functional terms this is certainly the correct way to view the *meng-* active; yet, as Verhaar observes (making the same point independently of both Givón and myself), the term "antipassive" is generally used for the construction with an oblique patient (Verhaar, 1982). In the variety of Malay under investigation here, it may be important that the affected patient of the ergative often has the "preposition" *akan* with it (see Section 2.1); if this "preposition" is viewed as a marker of the direct (i.e., accusative) case, then its absence might be taken as an indication of obliqueness, and the case for the antipassive interpretation of the *meng-* "active" would be complete.

4.4. *Event as Verb Focusing*

The characterization of the verb-initial clause type as eventive is supported by the distribution of the enclitic discourse particle *-lah,* which I have discussed in detail elsewhere (Hopper, 1979a, 1979c). This particle is not restricted to verbs, but serves to single out any major element of the clause. In the following passage, for example, the pronoun *aku* is in focus:

maka sampai- lah   ka- tempat aku menulis, maka undur-   lah   aku
then came   LAH to place   I   write   and shrink-back LAH I
*karna   di-antara juru-tulis itu semua-nya **aku- lah**   sa'orang*
because among scribes   the all-of-them I   LAH one-person
yang terkechil, ya'ani muda
the smallest indeed youngest
'Then he came to the desk where I was writing, and I shrank back, for among all the scribes it was I who was the smallest and youngest.'   (82)

The addition of *-lah* to a NP invariably focuses that element in much the same way as the cleft sentence construction does in English (a parallel I have suggested in the translation). The use of the same particle with a verb results in the foregrounding of the entire clause, as is illustrated by the two other examples of *-lah* (*sampai-lah* 'he came', *undur-lah* 'shrank back') in the same passage. The particle *-lah* can be added to both transitive and intransitive verbs; with intransitives it is the usual way of expressing foregrounding, while with transitives it denotes some special focus on the event, giving it the sense of a "pivotal" happening.[3]

---

[3] It is striking that an exactly parallel use of a discourse particle is found in Cajonos Zapotec (Jones and Nellis, 1979). In this language, the particle *na'a*, when following a noun phrase, serves to bring the participant into focus, and, when following a verb, singles out the event as of special significance to the development of the discourse.

[85]

Paul J. Hopper

4.5. Word Order and Discourse Function

The three clause types discussed in this paper can be grouped in two ways, with different perspectives:

1. From the perspective of MORPHOLOGY, the passive and the ergative are grouped together by reason of the prefix *di-* and other trappings of "passive" morphology described earlier.
2. From the perspective of WORD ORDER, the passive is grouped with the active (*meng-*). In these two constructions it is normally the case that a NP immediately precedes the verb.

The discourse functions which correlate with these structural groupings have already been discussed. Passive and ergative have in common a strong tendency toward association with a referential patient. Passive and active share a propensity toward backgrounding of the event (state, description, etc.). Figures 1 and 2 suggest a schematization of the two groupings.

The function that is common to active and passive is essentially a global, discourse one. Backgrounding is essentially definable in terms of the discourse as a whole, rather than in terms of local clausal semantics. By contrast, the feature shared by passive and ergative — definiteness of patient — is a local, semantic one. The discourse function of backgrounding is a complex one, not reducible to a single semantic parameter, but sharing several Transitivity parameters. These parameters conspire to produce an effect of slower action, and hence a lessened intensity of change. It seems significant that the broader, global, functions of foregrounding and back-

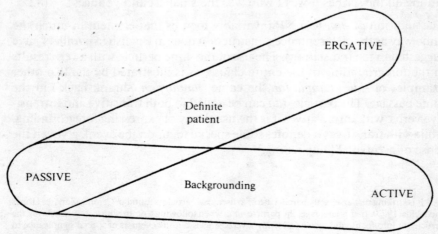

FIGURE 1. Functional grouping of the three major clause types.

[86]

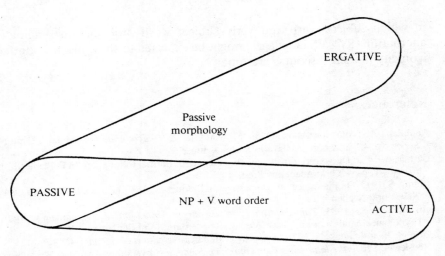

FIGURE 2. Structural grouping of the three major clause types.

grounding should be signaled by the less rigidly grammaticized, looser, device of word order, while the more restricted, local, function of definite patient should be signaled by the tighter, grammaticized, device of verb affixation. One might predict that this correlation (global discourse function — word order or other less grammaticized structure; local semantic structure — more rigidly grammaticized device) would represent a strong "iconic" tendency in human languages, if not a universal.

Finally, the fact that in the two backgrounding constructions a NP precedes the verb (agent in the *meng-* active; patient in the passive), whereas in the foregrounding construction (the ergative) the verb is initial, is also no coincidence: Narrative prose in Old English and Old Icelandic shows a precise parallel. In the Old Icelandic sagas, for example, verb-initial syntax is characteristic of a rapid tempo of narration, with events occurring in swift succession, usually in a series with the same actor, while subject – verb clauses — just as in Malay — slow down the tempo and serve to report background descriptions, explanations, and interpolations.[4] Both the Malay and the Icelandic styles use the positioning of a NP before the verb as a device for arresting the flow of the discourse and holding up the action by momentarily focusing attention away from ACTIONS to PARTICIPANTS, away from the dynamic HAPPENINGS to the THINGS (people and props) involved in those happenings. Languages such as Malay and Old Icelandic,

---

[4] See Heusler, 1967:170–171. The initial verb in Old Icelandic is characterized by Heusler as *bewegte Stellung* 'lively position', the post-subject verb as *Ruhestellung* 'rest position' (see also Hopper, 1975:51–52, 1979c:48–56).

in which subject – verb and verb – subject word order are in pragmatic alternation (SV – VS languages) might be expected to show just this kind of iconicity in their discourse grammar.

References

Abdullah [ᶜAbd Allāh ibn ᶜAbd al-Qadir 'Munshi']. 1932. *Hikayat Abdullah.* (Malay Literature Series No. 4.) Singapore: Malaya Publishing House.

Cartier, A. 1979. De-voiced transitive verb sentences in Formal Indonesian. In F. Plank (Ed.), *Ergativity.* New York: Academic Press.

Chung, S. 1975. On the subject of two passives in Indonesian. In C. Li (Ed.), *Subject and topic.* New York: Academic Press.

Givón, T. (Ed.). 1983. *Topic continuity in discourse: a quantitative cross-language study.* (Typological Studies in Language, Vol. 3.) Amsterdam: John Benjamins BV.

Grimes, J., and Glock, N. 1970. A Saramaccan narrative pattern. *Language* 46, 408–425.

Heusler, A. 1967. *Altisländisches Elementarbuch.* Siebente, unveränderte Auflage. Heidelberg: Carl Winter.

Hopper, P. 1975. *The syntax of the simple sentence in Proto-Germanic.* The Hague: Mouton.

Hopper, P. 1979a. Aspect and foregrounding in discourse. In T. Givón (Ed.), *Syntax and semantics 12: discourse and syntax.* New York: Academic Press.

Hopper, P. 1979b. Some discourse origins of ergativity. *Hawaii Working Papers in Linguistics* 11, 137–153.

Hopper, P. 1979c. Some observations on the typology of focus and aspect in narrative language. *Studies in Language* 3, 37–64.

Hopper, P., and Thompson, S. 1980. Transitivity in grammar and discourse. *Language* 56, 251–299.

Jones, B., and Nellis, D. 1979. A discourse particle in Cajonos Zapotec. In L. K. Jones (Ed.), *Discourse studies in Meso-American languages.* Arlington: SIL and University of Texas at Arlington.

Morgan, J. 1981. Some observations on discourse and sentence grammar. *Studies in the Linguistic Sciences* 11, 137–144.

Verhaar, J. Forthcoming. Ergativity, accusativity, and hierarchy. *Sophia Linguistica.*

PART II

Entities in Discourse

CHAPTER FIVE

Referents and Topic within and across Discourse Units: Observations from Current Vernacular English

Benji Wald

1. Introduction

The aim of this paper is to examine the role played by discourse, understood as coherent multisentence units in conversation, in the evolution of the syntax of reference. This general topic is addressed by investigating part of the English determiner system, namely, what has traditionally been called the INDEFINITE ARTICLES, as well as DEMONSTRATIVES in their unstressed attributive uses. It will become necessary in the course of the discussion to examine elements in the larger structure of discourse, in terms of the following concepts derived from syntactic–semantic and/or discourse studies: discourse unit, topic, and point.

At present, these concepts are not used to the same extent in different types of studies. The DISCOURSE UNIT has been discussed to various degrees of detail in studies of discourse as multisentential units in conversation (e.g., Linde, 1980; Wald, 1979; Silva-Corvalán, 1979), and it is implicit in a much larger variety of studies. The discourse unit represents a generalization from specific types of discourse units, of which the NARRATIVE as a unit expressing personal past experience is a particularly well-studied example (see Labov and Waletzky, 1967). The concept of TOPIC is much more widely used than is discourse in sentential syntax (cf. articles in Li, 1976), in semantic and philosophical studies (e.g., van Dijk, 1977), and in conversational studies (e.g., Keenan and Schieffelin, 1976). Of the three concepts, that of POINT is the least theoretically developed, but it is used in an

incipiently theoretical way, drawing on its common sense use as the PUR-
POSE or INTENTION of a particular stretch of speech.

As the discussion progresses it will become apparent that discourse and
syntactic studies offer a mutuality of opportunities, such that cross-fertiliza-
tion appears productive, even necessary, in accounting for the specific
phenomena of reference that will concern us here. Although it is my major
intention to investigate the effect of discourse levels of organization on
syntax, syntax as it has developed within sentential level studies, is in its turn
an indispensible tool for the analysis of discourse.

2. Determiners

In all current spoken and written varieties the paradigm of English
determiners includes the articles, of which *a/n* and *the* are traditionally
called *"indefinite"* and *"definite,"* respectively. The category article itself
bears further scrutiny, as it is not universal, and in some languages sentences
analogous to English sentences with articles may have either a demonstrative or no equivalent at all (e.g., Swahili, Chinese, Old English). However,
there is a well-known historical relationship between demonstratives and
articles in European languages that developed an article paradigm (including the Germanic and Romance languages). A formal survival of this
relationship in English is the noncooccurrence of demonstrative and article
modifying an NP, for example,

(1)   *a this one/   ?? this a one*
        *the that one/   *that the one[1]

English articles are distinguished from the demonstratives in lacking
pronominal uses, as shown by the following contrast:

(2)   *Did you see* $\begin{Bmatrix} that/one \\ *the/*a(n) \end{Bmatrix}$?

Historically, this distinguishing property is a result of the evolution of the
articles *the* and *a/n* in an unstressed context; the pronominal uses require
some degree of stress. On the other hand, both the articles and the demonstratives (used adjectivally) can occur in unstressed contexts.

Our concern will be specifically with the determiners associated with
indefinite specific reference in unstressed contexts. The recent evolution of

---

[1] This restriction is not true of all article languages. For example, vernacular Spanish allows the
construction ART–N–DEM, as well as DEM–N, as in *el muchacho este* (this boy) alongside *este
muchacho,* although not *ART–DEM–N or *DEM–ART–N (**el este muchacho*) (see Klein-Andreu, this volume, on adjective placement in attributive constructions).

the indefinite paradigm includes a striking innovation, which appears to have no precise analogue in other languages and yet indicates the effect of larger properties of discourse organization which themselves appear to be widespread, perhaps even universal, among languages.

3. Indefinite Specific Reference

In standard, especially written, varieties of English, indefinite specific reference of count nouns is indicated by *a/n* with singular nouns, and $\emptyset$ or *some* with plural nouns:

(3)　　a.　*I saw **a** man/**an** apple.*
　　　　b.　*I saw (**some**) men/apples.*

What the use of *some* adds to the determination of its noun is of more than passing interest. Generally, it is viewed as partitive, partitioning the class (generic) referent of the noun to include only a selected (usually indifferently, when *some* is unstressed) set of possible referents of the noun in the proposition. That is, *I saw some men/apples* implies that I did not see all/other men/apples. In contrast, the zero determiner allows either this partitive interpretation or a generic one, although the generic use is not necessarily equivalent to ALL, men/apples, but to ANY group of individuals which can be referents of the noun as exemplars (cf. Langendonck, 1980). This choice of use or nonuse of a determiner does not apply to singular count nouns. An article is obligatory in this case, whether the referent is specific, or an exemplar, or generic in some other way:

(4)　　*Specific:*　　*There was an/*$\emptyset$ apple on the ground.*
　　　　Generic:　　*An/*$\emptyset$ apple a day keeps the doctor away.*
　　　　Exemplar:　*This is an/*$\emptyset$ apple.*

(The sentences without a determiner suggest a mass rather than a count — individuating — referent for the noun. The use of *a/n* preserves its numerical origin of *one* in representing only countable referents.)

What has been said thus far is no less true of spoken English than it is of the written standard. However, varieties of spoken English (English vernaculars) also include other indefinite determiners, which are rarely exemplified in written English. These further indefinite determiners are unstressed *some* (hereafter *sm*) with singular count nouns and unstressed *this/these* with singular and plural count nouns. Of these two, the use of unstressed *this/these* to introduce indefinite specific referents is a more recent, and in some respects more striking, development in the determiner system of vernacular English. This use of the determiner *this/these* will hereafter be referred to as "new-*this*," for reasons explained in what follows.

[93]

4. New-*this*

There are several ways in which the "newness" associated with new-*this* is of great linguistic interest. First, new-*this* is widespread among vernaculars in both the United States and England, and yet it is relatively new in origin. Although it has been treated for various purposes in studies dating back to the 1950s (discussed in what follows), there is no known record of its use before the 1930s. If this origin is as recent as it looks, new-*this* is an innovation that has enjoyed phenomenal geographic expansion in the twentieth century. Social constraints on its use are much in evidence. It is not generally found in written English, unless to represent colloquial speech. Ochs (1979) observes that speakers who used it in speech changed to *a/n* (plural *some*) in producing written versions of the same narrative events:

(5) Spoken: . . . *there were* **these** *people talkin n* **this** *woman lady*
     [sic] *was describin somethin.* . . .
  Written: . . . *and* **a** *woman whose back was turned toward me as*
     she wildly conversed with **some** *friends.* . . . (Ochs,
     1979:69)

Rare occurrences of new-*this* in written English betray its spoken origin. The following example in a journalistic style of English is interesting because of the use of new-*this* in indirect speech.[2]

(6) *Near the end of it Baldwin made one request of Nelson. What was*
  it? the reporter asked. Well, said Baldwin, he had **this** *girlfriend*
  out in Wisconsin, and perhaps Nelson could refer to him in his
  story as a husky ex-Marine. (Halberstam, 1979:891)

It is informally observed that new-*this* is also more common among children and adolescents than among adults. Whether this is a generational manifestation of a change in progress, or simply a reflection of a stable age-grading phenomenon, perhaps associated with elaboration of styles in approaching adulthood, remains unclear. In any case, the recentness of new-*this* in

---

[2] The use of new-*this* seems to be expanding in those styles of journalism most open to spoken innovations. Even while I have been revising this paper, further examples have appeared in news magazines; for instance:

 (i) *Bob Selig was at a party back in Northern State University in South Dakota, feeling bruised*
  and lonely, and **this** [emphasis mine] *girl wouldn't let him alone. "Did you kill people?" she*
  kept asking. . . . (Newsweek 12/14/81:96)

It is consistent with the findings reported in the text of this paper that the girl, first mentioned in the citation given here, is referred to five times in the course of the article, including four times in subject position. It is likely that the writer derived this report from a recorded narrative by Bob Selig, in which he actually used new-*this* to introduce the girl.

contrast to *a/n* or *sm* is beyond dispute. Both of the latter have figured in English since at least the twelfth century, at which time *a/n* expanded in the written language at the expense of *sm*. (Mustanoja, 1960:260ff., places the final disappearance of written *sm*, i.e., *some*, with singular count nouns, in the thirteenth century, but it is listed until 1578 among the *OED* examples.)[3]

Another aspect of the newness of new-*this* bears directly on its discourse and syntactic functions. As the introducer of an indefinite specific referent, it indicates that the referent is new to the discourse. This function of signaling new information has been discussed for several determiners. For example, Hawkins (1978) considers the indefinite — including the singular indefinite specific *a/n* — to signal that the modified referent is not locatable among a shared set of individual referents at the given point in conversation. He refers in passing to new-*this* (calling it "introductory *this*"), as a stylistic variant of indefinite specific *a/n*. Prince (1981) develops a similar view in a discussion specifically addressed to new-*this* (called "indefinite this," as opposed to the definite uses of *this*, characteristic of all English demonstratives and their analogues in other languages). She proposes a set of familiarity constraints which distinguish use of new-*this* from *the;* as in Hawkins (1978), this distinction involves the notion of a referent already shared by participants to a conversation.

The fact that new-*this* is constrained to specific referents is reflected in its obligatory pronominalization as a definite, rather than indefinite, pronoun:

(7) a. *Roxie wants to marry a/this linguist$_i$, if she can find him$_i$.*
     b. *. . . a/*this linguist$_i$ . . . one$_i$.*

There is no such constraint on *a/n*, as (7b) shows. It is transparent to a specific – nonspecific distinction, registering only countability as an individual referent. The inability of new-*this* to introduce a nonspecific referent, as demonstrated in (7b), reflects the continuity of its character as a demonstrative.

However, the generalization of a specific marker, such as the demonstrative, from definite to indefinite uses is not well attested among historical processes in language. It is true that some syntactic constructions in other

---

[3] With singular count nouns, *sm* remains in common use as a direct descendant of 'some NP or other', where the speaker either does not have much knowledge of the referent, or wants to minimize its distinctiveness for some other reason, as in " . . . we were going up Atlantic Boulevard . . . when the — *sm* woman made a lefthand turn in front of us . . . the officer that was driving [the car I was in] swerved with her or . . . I woulda been in my third accident in a half an hour [CB 57m, LA]."(See Footnote 4 for an explanation of the credit.) It was with great interest that I discovered one speaker, JR, among the late preadolescents, who characteristically uses *sm* for new-*this*, for example, "you know, there's *sm* girl, *her* name is E . . . one day *she* . . . " JR never used new-*this*. Whether or not this is a direct descendant of the same use of *sm* in Old English and early Middle English is problematic.

languages show a similar evolution: For example, the object marker in Swahili, which was originally an optional marker of a previously established referent, is currently in many urban vernaculars used with new human referents (Wald, 1979); in some Bantu languages, the pre-prefix has passed from a definite to a specific, and further to a meaningless, marker of nouns (Wald, 1973; Givón, 1974); and an object marker accompanying preposed object NPs in Santiago Spanish, traditionally restricted to definite NPs, is now found to some extent with indefinite specifics and generics as well (Silva-Corvalán, 1981). In none of these languages, however, nor in others for which information is available is there another case of a demonstrative used with indefinite specific reference.

At this point we can examine the common properties of new-*this* in spoken discourse, leading to a discussion of the discourse effects on its evolution.

5. Discourse Features of New-*this*

The distinction between new-*this*, as a marker of a new referent, and unstressed uses of both the definite article *the* and the demonstrative *that/those* (abbreviated hereafter as *that*), can readily be seen in the following citation:[4]

(8)   . . . **these** *two girls$_i$, they were like playing hide-n-go-seek n* **this** *little boy$_j$ n* **this** *girl$_k$, they . . . came . . .* (all new referents in discourse up to this point) *n* **the** *little girl$_k$ went up there . . . all* **the** *girls$_i$, like they wanted to scare her, and* **that** *little boy$_j$, when they grew up . . . he wanted to get all* **those** *girls$_i$. . . .* (VS 12m, LA)

New-*this* introduces new referents which were not previously shared by the conversants. Once the referents have been mentioned they become shared. At that point, *the* or *that* is used with recurrences of the referents as lexical nouns.

The following segment shows variation between *a/n* and new-*this*.

(9)   . . . *there's* **a** *lady that went on a roller coaster. No, not really a roller coaster. You know Knotts Berry Farm,* **that** *thing that goes up? There's* **this** *lady that went on . . .* (CS 11m, LA)

---

[4] Unless otherwise noted, citations are from sociolinguistic interviews conducted by the author or under his direction. The citations for speakers 12 years old or younger are from research sponsored by the National Institute of Education and directed by the author for the National Center for Bilingual Research in Los Alamitos, California. The author is solely responsible for selection and interpretation of the data presented in this paper. (The abbreviation LA stands for the greater Los Angeles area.)

There are several points of interest here. First, the replacement of *a/n* by *this* in the reintroduction of the referent *lady*, is not clearly new-*this* in the strictest sense of first mention. However, the use of the existential clause, associated with the introduction of a new referent in discourse, suggests that *this lady* is to be taken as a new referent within the discourse unit (a narrative about an event the speaker witnessed at Knotts Berry Farm). This is an important point which will be amplified in ensuing discussion of the organizational boundaries within and across discourse units. In passing, it is noteworthy that *that* introducing the referent *thing that goes up* directly appeals to culturally shared knowledge. This includes it among definite referents, according to traditional notions and the current characterizations of definiteness as a shared set of referents (cf. Hawkins, 1978; Prince, 1981).

A search for a distinction between new-*this* and *a/n* within indefinite specific contexts has led some observers to posit further features of discourse intuitively felt to characterize the choice between these two indefinite determiners in specific contexts. Gleason (1965:348) mentions the vividness and topicality of new-*this* as opposed to *a/n*. Gleason appears here to imply a connection between new-*this* and *this* used definitely to introduce the first mention of a referent in the here-and-now (i.e., in the speech situation), termed EXOPHORIC reference by Halliday and Hasan, 1976:

(10)   *Look at this mess!*

The implication of vividness is similarly found in discussions of new-*this* by Lakoff (1974) and Maratsos (1976:134). It may also be pointed out that it is not unusual for stand-up comedians to begin jokes with new-*this*, as in *There was this farmer's daughter.* This opening is characteristically followed by use of the "historical present," which is also traditionally associated with vividness: *So one day this traveling salesman comes around* (cf. Schiffrin, 1981). However, it is far from clear that vividness refers to anything other than the grammarian's reaction to a form that is stylistically constrained to colloquial speech (cf. Wolfram, 1980). Thus, a direct relationship between new-*this* and unstressed spatial (exophoric) *this* is suspect, if it implies a closer relation between these two uses than between new-*this* and other uses of unstressed *this*, discussed in what follows.

We will indeed encounter other uses of unstressed *this* that suggest the foregrounding of a referent for extended attention. These are closely associated with topicality.

The notion of topicality of a new-*this* referent, mentioned by Gleason, is further developed by Perlman (1969). Perlman suggests that introduction of a referent by new-*this* implies that MORE INFORMATION about the referent is imminent as the discourse progresses. He intuits that a new-*this* referent in discourse typically includes a modifier and/or other adjuncts, such as relative clauses, that add further information about the referent. He further proposes that the use of *a/n* rather than new-*this* in the following imagined exchange is coy, as, in contrast to the use of new-*this*, it suggests that further information will be withheld.

(11)   Man: *Who gave you the mink coat?*
        Woman: ***This/a friend.*** (Perlman, 1969:79)

The value of this last proposal is unclear in view of the following exchange recorded during one of our sociolinguistic interviews.

(12)   BW: *Who's your best friend?*
        JF: ***This guy.*** (referring to no one present)

At this point JF offered no further information, and his peers chuckled, presumably at the vagueness of his response (as if he were withholding further information).

However, in general, Perlman's intuitions are borne out by speech data. In data from 19 preadolescent (10–12-year-old) new-*this* users, referents introduced by new-*this* typically received further mention, and were favored over *a/n* in sentence types that either included immediate adjuncts or were associated with topicality, especially SUBJECT contexts, with or without left dislocation:

(13)   a. Relative clause adjunct:
           . . . *n there's **this** guy that goes into the next door neighbors'es*
           house. (MR 12f, LA)
        b. Subject:
           . . . ***this** one girl was sayin', don't do that!* (IP 12f, LA)
        c. Left-dislocated subject:
           . . . *once **this** boy, he beat up my brother.* (EP 11f, LA)

Existential clauses, usually with adjuncts giving further information about the referent, are common, as in (13a).[5]

Table 1 shows the extent to which new-*this* is favored over *a/n* in all three syntactic frames, for this sample of 19 speakers.

Although the syntactic frames in Table 1 show a link between topicality and new-*this* (further discussed in what follows), it should be noted that topical referents are also introduced in object frames, especially after the verbs *have* and *know*, often with a recurring reference in an immediately

---

[5] Although the NP of the existential clause is sometimes considered its "subject," it is excluded from subjects in this paper. The most important reason is that it necessarily follows its verb in speech. Its claim to subjecthood is also tenuous on the basis of verb agreement. Generally the verb of the existential clause (*be*) is singular regardless of the number of the NP, although even young speakers in the sample occasionally (but rarely) observe the standard agreement pattern.

TABLE 1.
*Percentage of New-*this *out of* New-This + A/n *for three Syntactic Frames*

LEFT DISLOCATION	SUBJECT	HEAD OF RELATIVE CLAUSE
100	83	73
($N = 8$)	($N = 12$)	($N = 15$)

following clause. The following examples show that the second clause may have a simple syntactic relation to the first:

(14)   a. Parataxis:
      *. . . they had **these** little kids$_i$; **they**$_i$'re about 10, 11 years old. . . .* (MC 12m, LA)
   b. Simple conjunction:
      *. . . like, in back of where I live my father knew **this** guy$_i$ n he$_i$ had two sons. . . .* (LM 16m, Boston)

In some cases of a recurring referent in an immediately following clause, regular rules of ellipsis suppress surface expression of the topical referent in the second clause:

(15)   *. . . **this** guy$_i$ had a gun n $\varnothing_i$ was gna shoot another guy. . . .* (MR 12f, LA)

Generally, theories of sentence grammar consider $\varnothing_i$ to more abstractly represent a further reference to the previous referent of *this guy,* replaceable by an anaphoric definite pronoun (e.g., *he*), if not by a full NP (e.g., *the guy*) introduced by a definite determiner.

     Features associated with topicality in discourse virtually insure that a topical referent, whether introduced by new-*this* or not, will recur within a larger discourse unit, even though we have seen that surface expression of implied recurrence of the referent may be subject to ellipsis under certain conditions [as in (15)]. The examples we have considered support Perlman's intuitions of the usualness of an immediate constituent relationship between a first clause which introduces a new-*this* referent and a second which adds further information about the referent. Now, however, we will examine the relation between topical referents and their recurrences at greater distances in discourse units. To this end, the special relation between discourse topics and syntactic subjects is of great interest, as subjects tend to be associated with GIVEN (shared), rather than NEW, information (cf. articles in Li, 1976, especially Givón). It is thus not surprising that *a/n* as an indefinite, introducing a NEW specific referent, is unusual in determining a subject (as in Table 1). By the same token, it is all the more noteworthy that a number of examples of new-*this* are found in the subject context. At this point we will consider evolutionary aspects of new-*this* in order to further understand why this is so.

6. Evolution of New-*this*

One possible historic source for new-*this* is unstressed *this* used anaphorically with individual human referents. Mustanoja (1960:174) notes the anaphoric use of *this*, "approaching the meaning of the definite article" in Old English, and continuing into Middle English, "particularly with personal nouns and names." Sentence-level examples are rarely sufficient to demonstrate that the referent is given rather than new. However, when we consider larger discourse contexts, we can see that *this* is commonly used to mark the SECOND lexical mention of a referent, for example, in Chaucer's *Canterbury Tales*. Mustanoja associates this use with vividness and (not surprisingly) the spoken language: "this usage, mainly a feature of vivid, colloquial, and often chatty style, is particularly common in Chaucer's and Gower's works [p. 174].[6]"

The scheme of the first and second lexical mentions of each of the four principal characters of Chaucer's "Miller's Table" illustrates the use of unstressed anaphoric *this* (that *this* in each instance is unstressed is revealed by the meter, cf. Halle and Keyser, 1966). The first and second lexical mentions are presented with the line identified, and THIS indicates unstressed anaphoric THIS.

(16) *Whylom* (=once) *ther was dwellinge at Oxenforde*   1
  *a rich gnof*ᵢ (=lout) *that geestes heeld to borde*   2
  . . .
  *With him*ᵢ *ther was dwellinge **a poure scoler**ⱼ*   4
  . . .
  *THIS clerk*ⱼ *was cleped* (=named) *hende* (=clever) *Nicholas.*   13

  *THIS carpenter*ᵢ *had wedded newe **a wyf**ₖ*   35
  . . .
  *Fair was THIS yonge wyf*ₖ . . .   47
  . . .
  *Now was ther of that chirche **a parish clerk**₁*   126
  . . .
  *THIS Absolon*₁, *that jolif* (=good-natured) *was and gay*   153

[6] Mustanoja (1960) fails to appreciate the distinction between anaphoric unstressed *this* and new-*this*, but rather refers to an example of new-*this* from a modern American novel as a continuation of the Middle English usage illustrated by Chaucer. He considers the current new-*this* use as "lively but less educated speech."

TABLE 2.
Recurrent Lexical References of the Four Main Characters in Chaucer's "Miller's Tale," according to Relation to Verb of Clause

LEXICAL REFERENT STRUCTURE	PERCENTAGE
All subject references/Subjects + objects	88% (70/80)
Unstressed *this* + subject/all subjects	63% (44/70)
Unstressed *this* + object/all objects	30% (3/10)

It is to be noted that Chaucer (or the miller who is telling this tale) always uses *a/n* to introduce a new referent. But once the referent is introduced, he uses unstressed anaphoric *this* with second lexical mention. Chaucer's representation of the speech of the miller is particularly striking in the extent to which unstressed *this* continues to recur in introducing further lexical references to these topical referents of the tale. The miller's bias in favor of using unstressed *this* with *subject* lexical recurrent references is seen in Table 2.

First, in the unit (tale) as a whole, lexical mentions of the main characters occur mainly when they are subjects. Second, unstressed anaphoric *this* is much more favored with lexical recurrences of the referent as subject than as object. The first point helps establish the effect of topicality on subject contexts, as opposed to other syntactic contexts. The second point indicates the special relationship of unstressed anaphoric *this* to subject position, and by implication to topicality.

The association of new-*this* with recurrent referent subjecthood is seen in current narratives. One current narrative, which will be examined in further detail in what follows, illustrates a difference between the new-*this* introduced referent and the *a/n* introduced referent, both human. The sentence in which the two referents are introduced, already given in (15), is repeated here for the reader's convenience;

(18)   . . . **this** *guy had a gun n was gna shoot* **another** *guy* . . .

This first mention of these two characters in the narrative of 12-year-old MR is followed by a series of recurrences of both referents. Table 3 counts all mentions of both referents, either lexically or as pronouns. Thus, although both referents show the same number of overt recurrences, the one initially modified by new-*this* recurs much more often as subject.

Although the recurrence of the new-*this* referent as subject in MR's narrative resembles the subject preference of unstressed *this* in the miller's speech, the actual repetition of unstressed anaphoric *this* in the miller's

TABLE 3.
Recurrence of the Two Human Referents in MR's
Narrative as a Ratio of Subject/Total Recurrences

this guy:	lexical recurrence	100% (5/5)
	pronominal recurrence	100% (7/7)
another guy:	lexical recurrence	50% (2/4)
	pronominal recurrence	38% (3/8)

speech is not paralleled in MR's narrative. The miller's pattern is most closely approximated by the following mock-narrative told by a Liverpool teenager, illustrating how to "talk hard."

(20)   . . . *I'm tellin ya the truth like, there's sm skinheads So we—we wen' up to **these** skinheads n kicked them in the fuckin gob, we did . . . we come out there n then we started kickin shite outa **these** skinheads, . . . n next minute **these**—twen'y a **these** skinheads come along. . . .* (RC 17m, Liverpool)

One might suggest a historical link between Chaucer and MR's use of unstressed *this*, as schematized in (21):

(21)   a. *a/n* R_i . . . *this* R_i . . . *this* R_i . . .
         b. *this* R_i . . . *this* R_i . . . *this* R_i . . .
         c. *this* R_i . . . Def R_i . . . Def R_i . . .
         (where the first R_i of each line is first mention of a new referent, and R_i is always lexical and as a whole favors subject contexts, and Def is any definite determiner)

According to this scheme, the first discourse pattern is the origin of the others. It is the style represented in the miller's speech. The second pattern simply extends this pattern to the first mention of the referent, in anticipation of its topicality. It is restricted to a style in which unstressed anaphoric *this* is used repeatedly—the style approximated by RC's "hard talk." MR's narrative style, typical of current speech, represents a further innovation in which intensive successive uses of unstressed anaphoric *this* are no longer stylistically required, but the topicality of the referent introduced by new-*this* is preserved. In this current style, any definitizer may introduce a subsequent reference to R_i.

It is important to note that this linking scheme of styles evolving in discourse is especially suited to accounting for human referents. The next section discusses new-*this* with nonhuman referents, and leads to consideration of the larger structure of discourse.

7. New-*this* and Inanimate Referents

The property of recurrence of NP referents marked by new-*this* extends to inanimates. Within discourse, inanimates introduced by new-*this* often recur overtly as in (22):

(22)   . . . *so I took off my jacket y'know n I had on* **this** *turtleneck sweater,* **it** *was a knitshirt y'know n everything of my brother's.* . . .   (CM 16f, Chicago)

Here we note that *this sweater* is immediately followed by a second mention in *it* as the subject of the immediately following clause. Example (22) is a segment from a fight narrative told by CM. Within CM's larger fight narrative, *this sweater* is a LOCAL topic, ranging over this subsection of the larger discourse unit.

Overt recurrence is not, however, an obligatory feature of the use of new-*this* introducing a referent. Locatives and temporals are frequently marked by new-*this* but seldom recur in overt form. An example of locative/temporal new-*this* occurs at the beginning of CM's discourse:

(23)   . . . *they went to* **this party** *and uhm — over at T's house.*

The reference to *this party* which establishes the locative and temporal boundaries of a number of events that follow in the discourse, is not itself repeated. Nevertheless, locative/temporal setting remains understood until there is an overt change, in this case, " . . . *so* **the next day** *we went up to* **Pulaski Street.**" Another example, which we will discuss in more detail later, is the following:

(24)   *I was in a car accident — n uh we were jus' goin by* **this** *intersection. There was a stop sign n uh we stopped. N we started up again n* **this** *car went right through n the — the — I was sittin next to the door, n the door came in against my leg, n my head went almost to the dashboard.*   (AB 17m, Boston)

This is an entire narrative by AB. Both referents introduced by new-*this* are mentioned only once.

Many linguists have observed that inanimate referents, in contrast to human referents, are less likely to become recurrent (see articles in Givón, 1979). Even human referents vary greatly across languages with respect to overt reference. Near one extreme is Swahili, which obligatorily verb encodes all subject referents, most of which are human (especially in narrative and other stories of general interest). Most human objects are also verb encoded in Swahili; nonhuman objects are verb encoded only when they are topical, which is generally indicated by their relatively frequent recurrence within the discourse unit (Wald, 1979). Spanish shows a similar tendency (Silva-Corvalán, 1981). At the other extreme is Chinese, in which even human referents are often totally unexpressed (Li and Thompson, 1979). Given this cross-linguistic variability of constraints on the expression of previously mentioned specific referents, a simple count of references to referents will not necessarily reveal their relative topicality. Even in English, a simple count of overt references to a referent first introduced by new-*this* will not invariably show a relation to IMPLICIT recurrence, or to sustained relevance. Locative and temporal referents are a case in point. Such referents, directly relevant to the topic, rarely recur; yet, in some covert way, they remain part of the understood setting until being overtly replaced by *new* locative and/or temporal referents.

In order to discuss further the relation of the determiner-marking of referents to topicality within larger units, it is necessary to examine the discourse concepts of topic and point as they relate to discourse units. This will be done in the following sections, with particular attention given to narratives, as discourse units that are extended, potentially syntactically elaborate, commonly spoken, and easy to elicit.

8. Topic and Discourse Unit

There have been numerous treatments of topic in syntactic and discourse studies. For the most part, they focus on the notion of "aboutness" in the sentence and larger units (see, e.g., discussion in van Dijk, 1977).

Sentence syntacticians have generally associated topic with an NP, usually the FIRST one in the sentence (cf. Chafe, Givón, and other authors in Li, 1976). Therefore, the topic might be the subject of the sentence as in (24), — *was in a car accident* . . . , or even a left-dislocated constituent that does not refer to the subject of the next clause, for example, *this girl, her name is N* . . . (YL 11f, LA).

This FIRSTNESS property of topics is also reflected in larger units, as a consequence of "aboutness." Where topic is associated with early NP referents which recur as subjects within the discourse unit (DU hereafter), the firstness property is clear. However, some discourse studies adopt a more specific notion of topic as a PROPOSITION linking at least one NP (abstractly "something") with an event or state of affairs (abstractly "happen") presented in the expanded form of a DU. Thus, Keenan and Schieffelin (1976) characterize the topic of conversation as "a proposition (or set of propositions) *about* [emphasis mine] which the speaker is providing or requesting new information [p. 338]." Adopting Keenan and Schieffelin's discussion to present purposes, a topic as a proposition has the general form "something happen," to which some tense and/or modality is added, for example, "something happen*ed*" with past reference, and "something happened involving *me*" in the case of narratives and eyewitness reports. Keenan and Schieffelin suggest that once the general conditions for a communicative exchange have been satisfied, the first work in establishing a discourse topic is the introduction of the referents of the proposition, such as the man with the gun in MR's narrative or the car accident in AB's. This view of topic is essentially that of an abstract sentence with a set of referents to be filled in from the lexicon. However, how many referents belong to the topic and how complex the proposition may be is left open. Logically proceeding from Keenan and Schieffelin's characterization, some approaches have suggested that a topic expands throughout discourse, incorporating all new information.

Keenan and Schieffelin's discussion of discourse topic is concerned mainly with the maintenance of topic over several rapidly alternating turns at conversation. It does not deal specifically with particular DUs, or, especially, with coherent multisentence DUs spoken by a single speaker. Floor-holding discourses such as the narrative can be described in terms of their own internal structure, as proposed by Labov and Waletzky (1967). Discussion of this approach suggests a use for the concept of propositional topic of a multisentence DU.

In summarizing the Labov–Waletzky scheme for narrative structure, Labov (1972) observes that, although a minimal narrative may consist of a sequence of narrative clauses (clauses iconically ordered according to the temporal sequence of events they represent), narratives not uncommonly begin with nonnarrative clauses containing information pertinent to the body of the narrative. Thus, a fully elaborate narrative has an abstract, providing a summary of the story to be narrated, followed by an orientation section introducing situational referents such as time and place of the events about to unfold. For our purposes, the abstract is of particular interest. Inasmuch as the abstract is actually a preview of the narrative, it tells what the narrative is *about*.

Thus, the abstract is an overt representation of the propositional topic of the narrative as a DU. In AB's short narrative, the topic of the DU was reflected in the abstract: *I was in a car accident.* Similarly, MR's narrative about the man with the gun begins with an abstract, and then shifts to events leading to the potential shooting (the other human referent was never actually shot, although he was shot at, according to the story).

(25)   ABSTRACT:
         . . . *this one day . . . this guy$_i$ had a gun n was gna shoot another guy$_j$.*

BODY:

cz he$_j$ wen' in his$_i$ house—to rob . . . n the guy$_i$ came out with something . . . he$_i$ ran all the way to a corner . . . n then the other guy$_i$ had the gun. They$_i$ (=he$_i$)* started to shoot at him$_j$ . . .

   *Although MR uses the plural pronoun *they* here, in context, the referent is clearly singular, as only one man with a gun is ever mentioned.

The abstract as propositional topic of a narrative, or other story-type DU, fulfills the firstness property of topic, as a constituent of the entire DU. Because the abstract is optional in narrative, many DUs may not overtly show the topic. The DU may begin directly with the introduction of NP referents (in an orientation section, favored location for existential clauses), or directly with a set of events (the body of the DU as a set of narrative clauses). In such cases (or even when the abstract is present), discourse preceding the DU is likely to indicate the propositional topic. This will be pursued further, since it is related to cues in discourse as to the end, as well as the beginning, of the DU.

Let us now look at the end of the DU, the most essential element of which is that the POINT has been achieved.

9. Point and Discourse Unit

In discourse studies, the notion of point has not received the kind of attention devoted to topic. Labov (1972) discusses point under evaluative devices used in narrative. He considers such devices, used to evaluate the events of a narrative, to be second in importance only to the iconic relationship between the actual events mentioned and the order in which they are expressed in the narrative. He characterizes the relationship between the evaluative devices used to make a point and the point itself as follows. "[Evaluative devices are] the means used by the narrator to indicate the point of the narrative, its raison d'être: why it was told, and what the narrator was getting at. There are many ways to tell the same story, to make very different points or to make none at all [p. 366]."

It would be difficult to recognize the end of a narrative without some indication of a point. Possibly this is why young students use a formulaic close to end their written narrative-like compositions:

(26)   *When I was little I went to Halloween. I saw a momy and a witch. I was dress like spiderman my big sister dress like a Italiana and my sister dress like a cat and my baby sister dress like a cat.* **The Very End.**   (JS 8m, LA)

In coherent conversation, the point is recognized by its matching with some previous piece of discourse to which it is responding. Let us call this piece of discourse the DISCOURSE ORIGIN of the ensuing DU. As an example, consider the larger context of the narrative DU produced by MR, of which the abstract was *this man had a gun. . . .* The discourse origin occurs in a conversation among four people: MR; an adult male interviewer, BP; and two of MR's friends and peers, VL and IP.

(27)   1 BP: *Does that* (reference to VL's previous DU) *happen where you live, M?*
        MR: *No, but—*
        VL: *Nothing happens where I live.*
  2 BP: *You don't live in the same barrio?*
        IP: *Yeah.*
        VL: *Yeah, but nothing happens on her street.*
        MR: *Yeah* (contradiction, not agreement) *one day, one day* (ABSTRACT) *This one day at 4 — 6 or 5 a clock in the afternoon, this guy had a gun n was gna shoot another guy* (ACTION) *he wen' in his house. . . .*

In the discourse origin of MR's DU, the more abstract propositional topic "something happen," is closely approximated by VL's statement in (27–2): *. . . nothing happens on her street.* MR seems to take exception to this statement in her DU, where the contradiction of *nothing* by "something" is supported by a dangerous and reportable event she had witnessed on her street. Similarly, in AB's car accident narrative — a response to the danger of death question, used in many sociolinguistic interviews — the abstract proposition "something happen" is filled with the particular "I was in danger of death."

We can now consider the point of a DU. As presented here, the point is a first possible end point of the DU, at which the common sense point has been made. The common sense point is the particulars of "something happened" which validate the speaker's claim from which the DU originates. The propositional topic in the form of an abstract is the speaker's claim, which is then elaborated in a more complex reported experience represented by the DU.

It should be clear that the obviousness of DU points may vary according to the cultural and personal experience of the hearer. However, there are usually various cues indicating the end of a DU. Some are phonological; yet other cues are more deeply implicated in the organization of discourse, of which we will be particularly interested in syntactic cues involving indefinite reference.

Consider now the continuation of MR's narrative to its end point, and beyond it to following discourse.

(28)   2 MR: ... *this guy had a gun n was gna shoot another guy. ... n then the policemen came n then they took im to jail n all that. Then they left the car* (= the getaway car) *right here n then somebody wen' over there n burned it.* (last clause spoken with falling intonation and slowing of speech tempo)

   3 BP: *You saw all that happening, yeah?*

   MR: *n the(n)*—

   4 BP: *you weren't afraid that you might get shot too in the crossfire?*

   MR: (new DU) *No, I was just standing by in my friend's house. I was talking to her. N then **this** man comes out with a gun. I was where V is n the man was right over there w*— ... *So **this** man started to*—*to shoot n I ducked down cz the man had the gun toward where I was.*

At the end of MR's first turn in (28–2), her phonological cues are followed by an open turn, taken by BP. Hence in her first turn MR has crossed the terminal DU boundary. She made her point, disposing of the human referents involved in the narrative, *this guy* and *another guy*. She continued to dispose of a *car* as well before she stopped.

Whether she could have or would have continued the DU after taking a long breath is not so germane to the notion of point as the reaction of other participants. In particular, the implicit acknowledgement of the point by BP in (28–3)–(28–4) leads MR to further develop the details of her topic.

In spontaneous conversation, the point is recognizable through a variety of cues, none of which invariably occur. For example, there may be a coda such as *that's it* (cf. Linde, 1981:106ff), or a falling intonation and slowing of the speech tempo finally lapsing into silence. In any event, the most important cue is in the following audience (or addressee) reaction. This is implicit in Labov's (1972) discussion of warding off the reaction *so what?* in constructing the narrative. The *so what* reaction, like the analogous Spanish *y que* ('and what') and Swahili *halafu* ('and then'), appears as an indirect evaluation by treating the unit as INCOMPLETE — because the POINT has not yet been reached, so that the DU should not have ended. This suggests that the point is the FIRST possible ending for the DU. A more direct evaluation, which does not suggest incompletion, but rather that the point is unsatisfactory, would be *who cares, that's nothing,* or the sarcastic *big deal.* Polanyi (1979) shows for one narrative that nonacceptance of the point may lead to its reformulation in negotiation with interlocutors. The reformulation may further elaborate the point or change it completely.

The consequences of continuing a topic after the point has been achieved may be seen on the syntactic level in the use of determiners for indefinite reference. This leads us to a discussion of the determiners in a discourse context beyond the DU.

10. Topic and Reference across the Discourse Unit

If the topic continues to develop after the DU has reached its point, certain pieces of information already mentioned in the DU may be recycled, in the course of being elaborated upon. This happened in MR's further conversation pursuant to her topic, in (28–4), repeated here for convenience:

(29)   *No, I was just standing by . . . n then **this man** comes out with **a gun**. . . . The man was right over there. . . . **The man** had **the gun** toward where I was. . . .*

Although the referents in boldface were both established in the preceding DU, here MR reintroduces the gun with *a/n,* the indefinite article.[7] The referent *gun* had occurred three times in the preceding DU, but it is only after this first mention in the NEW unit that MR reverts to definite reference:

(30)   *This man had **a gun**. . . . The other guy had **the gun**. . . . The man with **the gun** took that man outa the car. . . .*

The continuation past the DU point of AB's narrative shows an analogous pattern with respect to indefinite reference:

(31)   AB: *I was in a car accident . . . **this intersection** . . . **a stop sign** . . . my head went almost to the dashboard.* (stops talking)
       BW: *You go to the hospital?*
       AB: *Yeah.*

---

[7] In response to a question asked by both Carmen Silva-Corvalán and Ellen Contini-Morava, the following phonological considerations distinguish *with a gun* and *with the gun* in utterances such as (29) and (30): The phonological sequence *with a gun* had a voiceless fricative: [wɪθəgɪn]. For this speaker, and her community, only *with* + vowel results in a voiceless segment. The alternative *with* + *the* is realized as [wɪ(d)ðəgɪn], where the fricative is voiced rather than voiceless. This follows from the general rule of sandhi for *with* + obstruent sequences in this vernacular, which requires that a sequence with dissimilar voicing either drop the first segment or assimilate it in voicing to the second.

[109]

BW: *How did the accident* (= previous topic) *happen?*
AB: (New DU) *I don't think it was our fault. It's just that we stopped at **a stop sign** y'know. It was at **an intersection**. N they didn't stop. . . .*

The inanimate specific referents are reintroduced as if they were new, although they are known from previous discourse.

In examining various writings on indefinite specific *a/n*, I found no direct discussion of the use exemplified in the continuations of MR's and AB's topics beyond the original DU in which they were first introduced. However, Hawkins (1978) makes some remarks concerning the semantic distinction between definite and indefinite marking which are relevant. First, he notes that as conversation progresses, the speaker and hearer come to share a larger set of referents. These referents belong to a "pragmatic set" such that "the use of the definite article acts as an instruction to the hearer to locate the referent of the definite NP within one of a number of objects which are pragmatically shared speaker–hearer knowledge and the situation of the utterance [p. 17]." Thus, once a referent is shared and *locatable* in previous discourse, indefinite reference can no longer be used, as it would imply that the referent does not belong to the shared set. Hawkins then discusses a hypothetical example in which an elderly couple are reminiscing about an accident they had in their youth. One of them says, *Oh yes, I remember. There we were, completely helpless when a nice friendly policeman came rushing to the scene. . . .* Hawkins argues that, although definite marking is a possibility for the referent *policeman*, an indefinite article might be used in cases where, for example, "[the speaker] thinks that the hearer may have forgotten about the policeman, or alternatively he wishes to formally reintroduce this object to the hearer *by consciously ignoring previous discourse,* which took place so long ago anyway [p. 195]."

Although AB's doubts about the addressee's memory are a possibility in (31), memory limitations or distance in time between successive mentions of the referent cannot reasonably be the cause of MR's use of the indefinite in (28–4)–(29).

In both MR's and AB's examples, the inanimates appear to be sensitive to the change in the discourse unit. They seem to be defined as given (definite) or new (indefinite) within the confines of the immediate discourse unit. Another way of putting it is that the indefinite marking of referents known from a previous unit is actually a cue to the new unit, and marks the use of the old referents to make a new point.

In other words, referential marking allows indeterminacy of reference outside of the old unit. A speaker is not required to mark definiteness of a referent last located in the old unit. This means that anaphora may be tightly bound to a range within a discourse unit, ending with the point of that unit. The constraint against locatability, expressed by Hawkins, restricts indefinite specific reference only within the DU. Beyond that unit, it becomes possible again. This explains the examples of AB and MR, as well as Hawkin's example. In this last example, all five determiners are possible: *a/some/the/that/this nice friendly policeman came rushing to the scene.*

Schematically, the possibility of using an indefinite determiner with a referent that is shared by virtue of mention in a preceding DU may be represented as follows:

(32) $a/n \; R_i \ldots$ (Def R_i) $\ldots // \ldots \begin{Bmatrix} a/n \\ Def \end{Bmatrix} R_i \ldots$ (Def R_i) $\ldots$

(*where a/n* R_i is FIRST mention of a referent on EITHER side of the DU boundary //)

The DU boundary separates the mentions of R_i into two distinct units. This discourse property of the choice between definite and indefinite reference, as it operates formally in the selection of English determiners, suggests further sources for new-*this.*

11. Variability of Discourse Context

The substitution of *this* for *a – the* in the "second" first mention of any R does not distinguish new-*this* from anaphoric unstressed *this.* Indeed, in MR's continuation past the point of the first DU *man* is reintroduced with *this* at the same time that *gun* is reintroduced with *a/n.* It is not possible to recognize this as an instance of new-*this,* as opposed to unstressed definite *this.*

(33)   . . . *n then* **this** *man comes out with a* **gun.** . . . [=(29)]

Similarly, CS shows an ambiguous case of *this* following the seemingly narrative-breaking clause in (9), repeated here in (34):

(34)   a. *there's a lady that went on a roller coaster.*   (introduction of referent)
        b. *No, not really a roller coaster. You know Knotts Berry Farm, that thing that goes up?*   (break)
        c. *There's this lady that went on.* . . . (recycle of introduction of referent)

But perhaps Example (34) is not ambiguous, as the existential clause of (34a) or (34c) seems to require indefinite reference. In contrast, most sentences are like Example (33), in that they are ambiguous with respect to new-*this* when taken out of discourse context.

The ambiguity of unstressed *this*, as replaceable by *a* or *the*, in the first mention of an old referent in a new DU suggests a path through which unstressed *this* may have evolved to more patently NEW contexts in competition with *a/n*.

(35)   a. *a/n* R_i . . . (Def) R_i . . . // Def R_i

b. *a/n* R_i . . . (Def) R_i . . . // . . . $\begin{Bmatrix} a/n \\ this \\ the/that \end{Bmatrix}$ R_i . . .

c. $\begin{Bmatrix} a/n \\ this \end{Bmatrix}$ R_i . . .

Essentially, this scheme suggests that at the first stage, definitization is unbounded with respect to the DU. A shared referent may be determined by *this, that, the*, but not by *a/n*. At the second stage, determination is bounded by the DU so that a shared (old) referent may be treated as a new referent upon first mention in a *new* DU. Thus, *a/n* becomes a possibility for the marking of a "second" first mention. At this point *a/n* and unstressed *this* come into potential competition (but why *the* and *that* retain their greater distinctiveness from *a/n* will be explained presently).

At the third stage, the requirement of "second" first mention is dropped so that unstressed *this*, as well as *a/n*, may introduce a first mention in any DU, (and we will see that this also applies to *that/the* as well—but not in potential competition with *a/n* or *this*). At the same time, unstressed *this* retains its other features. It remains specific and indicates the topicality of its referent. Originally, the topicality would have been established in a preceding DU. As the constraint of a preceding DU no longer applies, the domain of topicality, for purposes of determiner choice, appears to become more narrowly restricted to the DU as a unit out of further context. The constraint which defines definiteness/indefiniteness in terms of a single DU, rather than across DUs, erases the condition that unstressed *this* may only introduce a referent that has been previously mentioned. No longer is there a distinction between "second" and "first" first mention, as first mention is strictly defined only within a single DU.

The extension of new-*this* to particular inanimates, not necessarily recurring in the DU as a whole, but tending nonetheless to express local topicality within the DU [cf. (22)], shows further generalization of new-*this* to smaller coherent stretches within the discourse. Topicality is registered in increasingly smaller domains, as new-*this* expands further into the domain of *a/n*, always preserving the specific interpretation it shares with the other uses of *this*.

A final note is in order on why *this* rather than the other unstressed definite determiners should have extended to indefinite uses by the device described here. In particular, it is worth discussing why the determiner *that*, which previously shared the property of second mention with unstressed *this*, would not have been a suitable candidate for such extension.

12. The First Mention Polarity of New-*this* and Unstressed *That*

It has already been shown that the topicality of referents introduced by new-*this* preserves a use of unstressed *this* that vastly predates the appearance of new-*this*. The relation to topicality has never been a property of the other definite determiners — *the* and its progenitor, *that*. It has long been obligatory that either of these latter be used for already shared referents within a DU. In addition, both have an important function when introducing first-mentioned referents. This function, captured by the locatability principle of Hawkins (1978) or the familiarity principle of Prince (1981), is to indicate that the speaker believes that the referent introduced by *the* or *that* is accessible to the addressee even in the absence of a previous mention. Typical examples involving *the* include *the sun, the moon, the president, the English, the end of time,* etc. The use of unstressed *that* is even more striking in the directness of its reference to expectedly shared information. We have already seen it in CS's *that thing that goes up* (*at Knott's Berry Farm*). The following is a particularly interesting example:

(36)   *My sister works in — you know **that** deer?*   (AL 12f, LA)

Shared information appealed to by the speaker allows the Hartford Insurance Company to be located as the referent of *that deer* (i.e., the information that the company symbol is an elk).

This particular use of unstressed *that* as a first mention is in striking contrast to new-*this* which anticipates a nonpresupposed topical referent. Given that the use of *the* and *that* to refer to information in a shared set of referents is longstanding (cf. Mustanoja, 1960:170), these determiners were apparently preempted from extending to the use inherent in new-*this*. On the contrary, unstressed *this* has never been commonly used in this way (as evidenced by the historical derivation of *the* from *that* rather than from *this*), and first mentions of the type *you know **this** deer/**this** thing that goes up?* have not been observed among new-*this* speakers.

Had *that* been extended to introduce the first mention of nonpresupposed referents, it would have lost its ability to indicate the speaker's expectation of the prior sharedness of a referent — an ability of great utility in discourse, and especially critical in the case of the first mentions of referents.

It should be clear, then, that although the topicality of unstressed *this* facilitated its extension to nonpresupposed first mentions, the already established use of the other determiners to indicate the presupposed status of a referent, whether as a first mention or not, prevented them from extending to a simple topicality function. To put it most simply, *the* and unstressed *that* already had an important use in the context of first mention of a referent before unstressed *this* acquired one, in the guise of new-*this*.

13. Concluding Remarks

The study of discourse provides insight into the study of syntactic systems by uncovering suprasentential contexts that condition syntactic choice. These contexts show coherent organizational properties at the level of the discourse unit and beyond.

In the particular case discussed here, first mention is a special discourse context in which unstressed *that* and new-*this* are polarized. At the same time, the behavior of *a/n* shows that first mention as NEW information is not necessarily defined beyond the discourse unit, a unit beginning with a topic and ending with a point. The unstressed nature of all the determiners in the discourse uses discussed here is a consequence of the quasi-obligatory nature of choosing among determiners in speech, of the fact that a determiner must be chosen to introduce an individual referent. The relation of new-*this* to topicality suggests the syntacticization of topicality in spoken English discourse within the determiner system. It may well be, as Perlman (1969) suggested, that English has been developing a "third article." However, it should also be noted that the distinction between articles and UNSTRESSED demonstratives is not particularly clear, unless discourse factors larger than the sentence are taken into account. Further examination of the function of reference systems in discourse should lead to a greater understanding of the dynamics involved in the development of article languages from the ubiquitous demonstrative type of language, and of the discourse requirements that propel further evolution within article languages.

Acknowledgments

An earlier version of this paper was presented at a preconference session at the Georgetown University Round Table in Languages and Linguistics on March 19, 1981. I would like to thank the participants and attendants of that conference for helpful and stimulating discussion. Without intending lack of acknowledgement of the numerous people from whose discussion I have profited in the preparation of this paper, I would especially like to express appreciation to John Gumperz, Jack Hawkins, Tony Kroch, William Labov, Charlotte Linde, Ellen Prince, Carmen Silva-Corvalán, Sandra Thompson, and Deborah Tannen. Of course, responsibility for the facts and interpretations in the present paper are strictly my own.

References

Givón, T. 1974. Syntactic change in Lake-Bantu: a rejoinder. *Studies in African Linguistics* 5, 117–140.

Givón, T. (Ed.). 1979. *Syntax and semantics 12: discourse and syntax.* New York: Academic Press.

Gleason, H. 1965. *Linguistics and English grammar.* New York: Holt, Rinehart & Winston.

Halberstam, D. 1979. *The powers that be.* New York: Dell.

Halle, M., and Keyser, S. J. 1966. Chaucer and the study of prosody. *College English* 28, 187–219.

Halliday, M. A. K., and Hasan, R. 1976. *Cohesion in English.* London: Longman.

Hawkins, J. 1978. *Definiteness and indefiniteness: a study in reference and grammaticality prediction.* Atlantic Highlands, N.J.: Humanities Press.

Keenan, E., and Schieffelin, B. 1976. Topic as a discourse notion. In C. Li (Ed.). *Subject and topic.* New York: Academic Press.

Labov, W. 1972. *Language in the inner city: studies in Black English Vernacular.* Philadelphia: University of Pennsylvania Press.

Labov, W., and Waletzky, J. 1967. Narrative analysis. In J. Helm (Ed.), *Essays on the verbal and visual arts.* Seattle: University of Washington Press.

Lakoff, R. 1974. Remarks on this and that. In C. Fillmore, G. Lakoff, and R. Lakoff (Eds.), *Berkeley Studies in Syntax.* University of California, Berkeley.

Langendonck, W. van. 1980. Indefinites, exemplars and kinds. In J. Van der Auwera (Ed.), *The semantics of determiners.* Baltimore: University Park Press.

Li, C. (Ed.). 1976. *Subject and topic.* New York: Academic Press.

Li, C., and Thompson, S. 1979. Third-person pronouns and zero-anaphora in Chinese discourse. In T. Givón (Ed.), *Syntax and semantics, 12.* New York: Academic Press.

Linde, C. 1980. The organization of discourse. In T. Shopen and J. Williams (Eds.), *Styles and variables in English.* Cambridge, Mass.: Winthrop.

Maratsos, M. 1976. *The use of definite and indefinite reference in young children: an experimental study in semantic acquisition.* Cambridge: Cambridge University Press.

Mustanoja, T. 1960. A Middle English syntax. Helsinki: Societe neophilologique.

Ochs, E. 1979. Planned and unplanned discourse. In T. Givón, *Syntax and semantics, 12.* New York: Academic Press.

Oxford English Dictionary. 1979. Oxford: Oxford University Press.

Perlman, A. 1969. This as a third article in American English. *American Speech* 44, 76–80.

Polanyi, L. 1979. So what's the point? *Semiotica* 25, 207–241.

Prince, E. 1981. On the inferencing of indefinite-*this* NPs. In A. Joshi, B. Webber, and I. Sag (Eds.), *Elements of discourse understanding.* Cambridge: Cambridge University Press.

Schiffrin, D. 1981. Tense variation in discourse. *Language* 57, 45–62.

Silva-Corvalán, C. 1979. *An investigation of phonological and syntactic variation in spoken Chilean Spanish.* Unpublished doctoral dissertation, University of California, Los Angeles.

Silva-Corvalán, C. Forthcoming. Semantic and pragmatic factors in syntactic change. In J. Fisiak (Ed.), *Historical syntax.* The Hague: Mouton.

van Dijk, T. 1977. *Text and context: explorations in the semantics and pragmatics of discourse.* London: Longman.

Wald, B. 1973. Syntactic change in the lake area of Northeast Bantu. *Studies in African Linguistics* 4, 237–268.

Wald, B. 1978. Zur einheitlichkeit und einleitung von diskurzeinheitlen. *Sprachstruktur– Sozialstruktur: Zur Linguistischen Theorienbildung.* In U. Quasthoff (Ed.), Koenigsberg: Skriptor Verlag.

Wald, B. 1979. The development of the Swahili object marker: a study in the interaction of syntax and discourse. In T. Givón (Ed.), *Syntax and semantics, 12.* New York: Academic Press.

Wolfram, W. 1980. A-prefixing in Appalachian English. In W. Labov (Ed.), *Locating language in time and space.* New York: Academic Press.

CHAPTER SIX

On the Interaction of Word Order and Intonation: Some OV Constructions in Spanish

Carmen Silva-Corvalán

1. Background

It is generally agreed that Spanish is an (S)VO[1] language which allows freedom in the linear arrangement of the constituents in any given sentence as compared with, for instance, English, which is also "an SVO language [but] not a free word-order language [Green, 1980:597 – 598]." On the other hand, various linguists have observed that word order in Spanish is not free in an absolute sense but is controlled by discourse and pragmatic factors (Bolinger, 1954 – 1955; Contreras, 1976; Firbas, 1962; Hatcher, 1956). This paper presents additional evidence in support of these observations but it goes a step further in that it is based on data selected from recordings of conversational Spanish. This permits us to examine the interaction of word order and intonation as well as the uses that speakers make of these devices in speech.[2] The constructions to be discussed are of the OV*X* type illustrated in (1) and (2), where O may be a direct or an indirect object (DO and IO respectively). Examples (1) and (2) may be said to be variable occurrences of (3) and (4), with postverbal objects, given that they have the same referential meaning.

---

[1] The use of parentheses around S signals the variable expression of the subject.
[2] The data were collected through individual sociolinguistic interviews conducted by the author in Santiago, Chile, in 1978. The transcription of the intonation of the examples discussed here was also done by the author. Some transcriptions were controlled by other native speakers of Spanish.

(1) *La verdura te la llevan de Santiago.*
'The vegetables they bring them to you from Santiago.' (E,f,34)[3]
(2) *Padrastro tengo.*
'Stepfather I have.' (G,m,51)
(3) *Te llevan la verdura de Santiago.*
'They bring the vegetables to you from Santiago.'
(4) *Tengo padrastro.*
'I have a stepfather.'

My purpose here is to investigate the motives that may lead speakers to use the inverted order OV and to describe some of the functions of these constructions. It will be seen that the OV order may be exploited for several different communicative purposes, ranging from establishing discourse cohesion through a smooth transition from older to newer information to signaling that the object is contrary to expectation.[4] It will also be shown that intonation and word order interact in interesting ways, namely:

1. Certain objects are placed in initial position because the intonation contour of the sentence allows the speaker to assign pitch prominence to preverbal constituents that do not convey new information.
2. A special intonation contour (see Section 4) is assigned to constructions with preverbal Os to signal the O either as contrary to expectation or as new information.

The facts about intonation, word order, and meaning lead me to conclude that these levels of description may not be kept totally apart. Indeed, what is shown here is that it is the configuration of both word order and intonation that correlates with any given meaning.

Direct and indirect objects do not occur in preverbal position with the same frequency. In a sample of 3161 sentences containing a DO, only 214 (7%) DOs occurred preverbally, whereas in a sample of 475 sentences containing an IO, 205 (43%) IOs were preverbal. This different behavior responds to the different semantic features of the objects.[5] Over 90% of the IOs are definite and human whereas the opposite situation holds for DOs: only 15% are human and 36% are definite. The fact that IOs are frequently human and definite whereas DOs are more frequently nonhuman and indefinite may account, then, for the higher frequency of occurrence of IOs in preverbal position, a position that is associated with old information and

---

[3] Information identifying the speaker is given in parentheses: name initial, sex, age. Examples that do not provide this information were made up by the author.
[4] One interesting question that I do not attempt to answer in this article is why these different communicative purposes are served by the same word order configuration.
[5] The consequences of these semantic differences on the expression of coreferential clitic pronouns are discussed in Silva-Corvalán (1981).

therefore definiteness. Note also that definiteness and humanness correlate with TOPICALITY; that is to say, they are two of the features characteristic of the kinds of referents that people tend to talk about (cf. Chafe 1976; Duranti and Ochs, 1979; Givón, 1976; Hawkinson and Hyman, 1975; Hyman and Zimmer, 1976; Li and Thompson, 1976). These referents are usually coded as the subject noun phrase and placed preverbally. It is interesting, then, to observe that in Spanish IOs share many characteristics with subjects: Both are frequently preverbal, human, and definite; and both must agree in person and number with the verb (by means of a verbal suffix and a dative clitic pronoun respectively).[6] DOs, on the other hand, appear much more fixed in their position after the verb and they are frequently indefinite and inanimate.

The discussion in this paper is organized as follows: Section 2 concerns itself with the relation between preverbal Os and old information; Section 3 investigates the contrastive function of preverbal Os; Section 4 discusses focal Os and the notion of being contrary to expectation.

2. Old – New Information

Various studies of Spanish word order (see references in Section 1) have contended that the primary function of word order is the signaling of old and new information, or thematic and rhematic material, in such a manner that in one- and two-argument sentences, new information will be postverbal and old information preverbal. Old information has been defined as presupposed information (Bolinger, 1954–1955), or as information that the speaker assumes to be in the addressee's consciousness at the time of speaking (Chafe, 1976; Contreras, 1976). Both Chafe and Contreras postulate old and new as a dichotomy since, to them, it does not make sense to talk about elements that are more or less present in the listener's consciousness. Our data, however, indicate that OLD – NEW IS NOT A DICHOTOMY and that the referents of the various constituents MAY BE MORE OR LESS NEW WITH RESPECT TO ONE ANOTHER.

This concept of gradience may be compared with the Praguian notion of COMMUNICATIVE DYNAMISM (CD). Within the Functional Sentence Perspective theory, sentence elements may convey different degrees of CD, that is, they may be more or less new. In Firbas's words, in accordance with the linear character of language, "known elements are followed by unknown elements, or to put it more accurately, sentence elements follow each other

---

[6] For an examination of the constraints on the expression and placement of the subject in Spanish see Silva-Corvalán (1982).

according to the amount (degree) of Communicative Dynamism (CD) they convey, starting with the lowest and gradually passing on to the highest [1962:36]."

Our data support the claims that old – new information is a continuum and that the linear arrangement of the constituents in a sentence is sensitive to these different degrees in such a way that the constituents will be ordered along a scale of increasing newness. This is illustrated in the following passage:

(5)　I:　(a) *Así es que ¿cuál es el profesor o la profesora que más te gusta, por ejemplo?*

　　　T:　(b) *¿A mí?* (c) ***A todo el curso le gustaba una monja que se fue.***

　　　I:　*Ah, ya.*

　　　T:　*Tuvimos –* (d) *Era la profesora jefe, una monja que era bien amorosa que se llamaba Madre Inés.* (e) *La tuvimos el primer semestre y se tuvo que ir a España por a . . . hacer una . . . un congreso.* (f) *No sé a qué, a qué se tuvo que ir y todo el curso fue a Pudahuel y lloramos y todo.* (g) *Ahí quedó la media crema en el, en el curso* (h) ***porque esa monja la adorábamos,*** (i) *porque era tan amorosa.* (j) *Hacía clases de matemáticas y de física.* (k) *Generalmente son las, las, las, los ramos que más nos cuestan* (l) *y esa monja hacía todo lo posible para, para ayudarnos.* (m) *Nos hacía clases, o sea, nos hacía clases . . . después de cla–, de horas . . . para, para recuperarnos, ¡qué sé yo!* (n) *O sea, era bien amorosa.*

　　　I:　(a) So who's the teacher you like the best, for example?

　　　T:　(b) Me? (c) **The whole class liked a nun who left.**

　　　I:　Oh, I see.

　　　T:　We had – (d) She was the homeroom teacher, a nun who was very cute, whose name was Mother Inés. (e) We had her for the first semester and she had to go to Spain for . . . to do a . . . a congress. (f) I don't known why, she had to leave and all the class went to Pudahuel and we cried and everything. (g) That left a mess in the, in the class (h) **because that nun we adored her,** (i) because she was so cute (j) She taught mathematics and physics. (k) On the whole, they are the, the, the, the most difficult subjects (l) and that nun did her best to, to help us. (m) She taught classes, that is, she taught classes . . . after cla–, hours . . . to, to give us extra help. You know! (n) That is, she was real nice.　(T,f,16)

Example (5) is taken from a part of the conversation during which T and the investigator (I) have been talking about T's school. Segment (c), a sentence that answers the question in (a), illustrates the use of a preverbal IO. Segment (h) illustrates the use of a preverbal DO.

According to a dichotomous definition of old – new information, it does not seem to be possible to consider *a todo el curso* in (c) to be old information. An investigation of the discourse preceding the passage in (5) indicates that *a todo el curso* has not been referred to before, so it may not be assumed that the referent of this IO is in the listener's consciousness. The subject, *una monja que se fue,* provides the new piece of information required by the question in (a) and is, as expected, in postverbal position. But, if the IO is NOT old information, it should also be postverbal. The fact that the IO is preverbal suggests the possibility that it may be viewed as old information by the speaker. In fact, it appears possible to relate *a todo el curso* with the information given in the preceding discourse about the speaker's school. This association is possible because in the discourse situation, where the speaker is talking about her school, *the whole class* is a likely referent to come up in the conversation and it may be assumed to be identifiable by the listener through her knowledge of how schools are organized. In contrast, even though the speaker may be expected to refer to nuns in this situation (it is a Catholic school), 'a nun who left' is not identifiable by the listener, who could not be expected to know that there was a particular *nun who left.* Furthermore, the referent of *a mí* (the speaker), which is presupposed, appears to be included in the referent of *a todo el curso.* Note that the question asks for information about which teacher the speaker likes best. In her answer she includes herself as a member of her class and provides information about which teacher was liked the most by all the class. It may be said, therefore, that relative to each other, the referents of the IO (*the whole class*) and of the subject (*a nun who left*) in (c) are "given to different degrees." The amount of information conveyed by the IO is lower than that conveyed by the subject because the IO is less important to fulfilling the request in (a). Therefore, the IO is in preverbal position and the subject in postverbal position in (c).

The referent of the DO *esa monja* in (h) is old information, having been introduced and identified as 'Madre Inés' in the immediately preceding discourse. In contrast, the fact that the whole class adored her is relatively new in that it adds a new degree (from liking to adoring) to the students' feelings for the nun. Accordingly, the DO is preverbal.

Moving from the known (old) to the unknown (new) establishes discourse cohesion. It is not surprising, then, that when the referent of an O constitutes old information or may be inferentially related to the preceding discourse and thus assumed to be more given (old) than the other constituents, the O will be placed in initial position, as in (c) and (h).

Thus, IF OLD AND NEW ARE VIEWED AS A CONTINUUM, it is possible to explain the linear arrangement of the constituents both in sentences like (h), in terms of SIGNALING OLD VERSUS NEW INFORMATION, and in sentences like (c), in terms of SIGNALING AN INCREASING DEGREE OF NEW INFORMATION. In this view, one of the functions of preverbal Os is to establish discourse cohesion, that is, a link between the known and the unknown. This connecting function is not restricted to so-called free word order languages, nor only to speech. Green (1980), for instance, offers many cases of inversions in both written and spoken English whose function is to establish a connective effect.

Preverbal objects such as those in (c) and (h) have been considered to be the TOPIC of the sentence.[7] Here, I will refer to them simply as preverbal Os and will use the term DISCOURSE TOPIC to refer to what a stretch of discourse is about. Discourse topic is a holistic concept, that is, no single sentences or entities necessarily represent the discourse topic. Rather, it is created from the integration of information expressed in a stretch of discourse that may be impressionistically determined to have coherence of content.

Let us observe again Example (h) from Passage (5), repeated here for ease of reference:

(5h)   *porque esa monja la adorábamos*
        'because that nun we adored her'

The topic of the discourse illustrated in (5) is *the nun who left*, that is, the speaker's favorite teacher. The discourse topic is suggested by the question in (a), it is established in (c), and it is identified in (d). There is no doubt that this passage is about the class's favorite teacher and not about the whole class, even though *the whole class* is coded as the subject four times. The referent of the discourse topic, on the other hand, is not necessarily coded as subject. In (h), for instance, *that nun* is the DO and *we* (i.e., *the whole class*) is the understood subject. Both noun phrases could have qualified to be expressed preverbally in (h), but only *esa monja* is chosen for that position.

The speaker has an alternative option available to her, though: the placement of the old information DO (*esa monja*), deaccented,[8] in postverbal position, that is, after the new information. I will argue here that the

---

[7] A review of the linguistic literature on topics (cf. Chafe, 1976; Contreras, 1976; Givón, 1976; Hawkinson and Hyman, 1975; Hyman and Zimmer, 1976; Keenan and Schieffelin, 1976; Duranti and Ochs, 1979; Li and Thompson, 1976; Wierzbicka, 1975) shows that there is agreement about the fact that topics appear in sentence-initial position. There is also agreement to the effect that topic is a discourse notion, that is, it is associated with such discourse factors as givenness, contrast, frequency of reference, etc., whereas, for instance, subject is a syntactic notion, that is, it plays a role in such syntactic processes as verb agreement, equi NP deletion, imperative subject deletion, etc., even though subjects are frequently also considered to be topics.

[8] I use the term ACCENT in the sense proposed by Bolinger (1972) who states: "Stress belongs to the lexicon. Accent belongs to the utterance [p. 644]." In other words, individual items that are stressed may appear without any pitch prominence, or accent, in any given utterance.

speaker has placed the DO *esa monja* in preverbal position because the intonation contour of declarative sentences in Spanish allows her to assign pitch prominence[9] to this noun phrase, whose reference conveys no new information in this particular sentence but which is important in the discourse.

At this point, a few words about intonation are in order. The complete declarative sentence in Spanish has a falling contour with two points of prominence: a pitch peak toward the beginning of the sentence and a slight fall toward the end (Barrutia and Terrell, 1982:93; Navarro, 1966:61). This gradual falling contour with a string-final sentence accent characterizes examples that consist of only *one* phonological phrase or breadth group, and I will limit my discussion to them. These constructions typically transmit information, with no special overtones or assumptions, in response to a question, in descriptions, in narratives, etc. Accordingly, I will refer to their pattern of intonation as the INFORMATION CONTOUR; it is illustrated in Examples (6)–(8)[10]

(6) I: *Tu papá es – ¿Toca algún instrumento? ¿Le gusta e–?*
     T: *Antes tocaba el violín.*

     I: Your dad is– Does he play an instrument? Does he like–?
     T: Before he played the violin.   (T,f,16,Ch21,A:185)[11]

(7) I: *¿Y usted qué edad tiene ahora ya?*
     s: *Yo tengo sesenta años.*

     I: And how old are you now?
     s: I'm sixty years old.   (S,f,62,Ch38,A:66)

(8) *La sal ha formado unas especies de cráteres.*

     'The salt has formed something like
     craters.'   (H,m,33,Ch23,A:140)

---

[9] I am not concerned here with the phonetic nature of this prominence. For the purposes of this study, accent and different pitch-levels are determined on the basis of subjective impression.

[10] Boyce and Menn (1979) propose the same contour for "normal declarative sentences" in English.

[11] The information identifying the speaker (see Note 3) is followed by information that identifies the tape, and in some cases, the side and the tape counter number where the example occurs.

Note that the information contour normally has two accents or points of prominence, which are manifested phonetically as an initial pitch peak and a pitch fall preceded by a slight raising of the pitch at the end. In most cases, the point of the fall occurs on an item that introduces new information into the discourse. As I indicated earlier, I propose that the existence of this intonation contour is one of the motives for the preverbal placement of Os that do not convey the new information in a sentence but that, for reasons directly related to the content of the discourse, the speaker intends to assign intonation prominence to, that is, to accent.

Let us proceed to scrutinize this proposal by examining the OV constructions in the following passage:

(9) (a) *Yo cuidé una viejita antigua.* (b) *Era muy católica, muy pechoña.* (c) *Tenía una propiedad, casa antigua con viñas p'adentro, así, potrerillo.* (d) *Y ella tenía mucha arboleda, porque ella hacía injertos, injertaba los árboles frutales, así que tenía de toda clase de frutas. Los primeros duraznos que ella sacaba eran unos duraznos de, de la virgen que llamaba yo, duraznos muy ricos.* (e) *Y esa señora a mí me enseñaba a leer,* (f) *pero como yo era . . . de la cabeza tan dura, nunca aprendí.* (G and I laugh) (g) ***A rezar sí que aprendía.*** (h) ***Y esa viejita la cuidé yo.*** (i) *Porque primero murió el viejito, el esposo. El esposo de ella se iba pa' la cordillera así porque decían que tenía otra señora él por allá. No sé, pues, si sería verdad o no. Entonces él venía de– . . .* (j) *Ella tenía mucha lana de vellón, en sacos. Ella me enseñó a llenar camas, a hacer colchones.* (k) *Yo no sabía hacer eso.* (l) *Entonces, el viejito un día le robó dos sacos de lana para llevárselos a la otra mujer que tenía, pa' la cordillera. Y dicen que tenía mujer por allá.* (m) *Y ése . . . se llamaba Pedro S. él,* (n) *tenía dos carretas con bueyes.* (o) ***Y las dos carretas con bueyes las perdió.*** (p) *Seguro que la otra señora se las quitó, seguro.*

(a) I looked after an old lady. (b) She was catholic, very devout. (c) She had a property, an old house with vineyards in the back, like that, fields. (d) And she had a lot of trees, because she did grafts, she grafted on to fruit trees, so she had all kinds of fruit. The first peaches that she got were these peaches, the virgin's peaches as I called them, delicious peaches. (e) And that lady taught me how to read, (f) but as I was . . . so dumb, I never learnt. (G and I laugh) (g) **I did learn to pray though.** (h) **And that lady I looked after her.** (i) Because the old man died first, the husband. Her husband used to go to the mountains because they say that he had another woman there. I don't know if that was true or not. Then he came from– . . . (j) She had a lot of wool, in sacks. She taught me how to stuff mattresses, to make mattresses. (k) I didn't know how to do that. (l) Then, the old man one day robbed her of two sacks with wool to give them to the other woman he had, in the mountains. And they say that he had a woman there. (m) And that man . . . he was called Pedro S., (n) had two oxcarts. (o) And the two oxcarts he lost them. (p) Surely the other woman stole them, surely.   (G,m,51)

Example (9) is taken from a conversation with G. Here, G is talking about an old lady who played an important role in his youth. *The old lady* is established as the topic of the discourse in (a) and coded as the subject every time this referent is mentioned from (b) through (e). It reappears as the DO in (h), and is placed in initial position because it is being reintroduced as the topic of the discourse and the speaker intends to mark it as a CENTER OF ATTENTION.[12] Independent justification for this interpretation of the speaker's intent is provided by the fact that *the old lady* is referred to 10 times in (a)–(h), whereas the second most mentioned referent, the speaker himself, is referred to 7 times, and *the peaches,* the only other referent that is mentioned more than once, is referred to only 3 times.[13]

A comparison of (9n) with (9o) will further illustrate the combined effect of preverbal placement and information contour:

(9n)   *tenía dos carretas con bueyes*

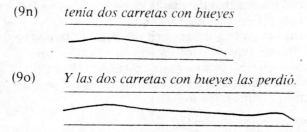

(9o)   *Y las dos carretas con bueyes las perdió.*

In both (9n) and (9o) the final accent falls on the rightmost element of the rightmost constituent that conveys new information, that is, on *bueyes* (9n) and *perdió* (9o). It may be argued that the preverbal placement of the DO in (o) responds to the older information first principle. But a postverbal DO would have also been acceptable as a continuation of (9n) if said on a low pitch after the accent on the verb. It would have been possible also for the

[12] Note that the Universal Hierarchy of Topicality proposed by Givón (1976:152), according to which the subject and/or a first person referent are more likely than the DO and/or a third person referent to be the topic of the sentence (i.e., sentence initial), is superseded by third person DOs whose referents are the topic of a stretch of discourse [see also Example (5h)].

[13] On the basis of an analysis of case assignment in German, Zubin (1979) has similarly concluded that "the frequency with which a speaker mentions an entity in a given stretch of discourse is a measure of the prominence of this entity in the speaker's discourse plan [p. 483]."

speaker to refer to *las dos carretas con bueyes* in (9o) only anaphorically, as in (9o'):

(9o')   *Y las perdió.*
'And he lost them.'

However, neither of these two alternatives, postverbal placement and anaphoricity, would have accomplished the same effect of calling the listener's attention to *las dos carretas* since the DO could not have been assigned intonation prominence. Anaphoric reference, lack of stress, and low pitch are defocusing devices. In a situation where the speaker wants to assign intonation prominence to a particular referent which does not convey new information, in order to draw the listener's attention towards it, he can place it in sentence-initial position. As I showed earlier, in this position the neutral information contour allows old information to be assigned a relatively high pitch. Thus, preverbal placement plus intonation converge to signal that an otherwise presupposed, deaccented referent is a reference point for the predication and a center of attention in the sentence and within a discourse passage.

It is clear that G does not feel much sympathy for the husband, and even less for the other woman. He conveys this lack of sympathy by calling to the addressee's attention the two oxcarts that the man had, probably all he had, and the fact that they were stolen by the other woman.

A further type of construction with a deaccented preverbal O should be introduced at this point. In this type of construction there is deaccented material in initial position, referred to as PREHEAD (Ladd, 1980:Ch.1). When an O occupies this deaccented initial position it appears to function simply as a DISCOURSE LINK, as illustrated in (10b):

(10)   a. *¿Y a tí te llevan al teatro a veces?*
        b. *No, a mí nunca me llevan.*

        a. 'And do they take you to the movies sometimes?'
        b. No, they never take me.'
           Lit.: 'No, to me never me take.'

3. Focus of Contrast

In (9g) there is an infinitival O in sentence-initial position, *a rezar* 'to pray', which introduces new information into the discourse. It is clear that this object is being contrasted with 'to read' (the speaker never learnt to read but he learnt to pray). This evidence leads me to hypothesize that an object that is a focus of contrast is placed in initial position. In this initial position this element may be assigned high pitch, the information contour need not be altered, and a meaning of 'focus of contrast' rather than simply 'new information' is assigned to it. A postverbal object may also be the focus of contrast, but in this position it must be assigned a special contrastive accent with a steep fall of the pitch. It is my contention, therefore, that if an O in an apparent situation of contrast occurs postverbally with string-final sentence accent but no special contrastive accent, it only conveys new/newer information, that is, the speaker does not intend to present it as contrastive. These two possibilities of signaling contrast are illustrated in (11) and (12):

(11)   *Realmente a los hijos, tú les das todo sin esperar nada.*

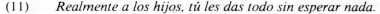
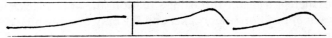

'Really to your children, you give them everything without expecting anything.'   (E,f,34,B)

(12)   a. *Yo no le hago nada, señora Carmen, al M., nada.*

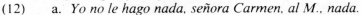

'I don't do anything, Mrs. Carmen, for M., nothing.'

b. *Nada, nada, nada.* c. *Todo le hace su madre, sus hermanas.*

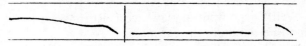
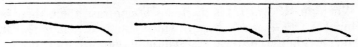

'Nothing, nothing, nothing. Everything his mother does for him, his sisters.'   (A,f,38,A)

Example (11) illustrates a case where two DOs, *todo* and *nada* are being contrasted with respect to *dar* 'give' and *esperar* 'expect'. They are placed in new information postverbal position where they would have been assigned sentence accent, that is, a point of intonational prominence, in this case the point of the pitch fall. Instead, they receive a special contrastive accent with a steep fall of the pitch because the speaker intends to present them as the foci of contrast. In (12c), on the other hand, where *todo,* contrasted with *nada,* is placed preverbally, it is assigned high pitch but no special contrastive accent.

The speaker has, then, two options to signal an O as a focus of contrast:[14] preverbal placement accompanied by high pitch, or postverbal placement with special contrastive accent. The data indicate that preverbal placement is a much more frequent option.[15]

At this point it is necessary to state explicitly what I mean by FOCUS OF CONTRAST. I call a noun phrase the focus of contrast when its referent stands in opposition to a closed number of alternatives that are clearly identifiable as members of the same semantic set. The notion of alternatives IN OPPOSITION, not just a list of alternatives, in that only one of the alternatives may be chosen as the right one with respect to a contrasting situation, is crucial to the definition of contrast.

For example, (13b) is simply a list of alternatives which are not strictly in opposition because there is no contrasting situation. In (14a)–(14b), on the other hand, there is a clear contrasting situation (the fit of a jacket) and two alternatives in opposition (the speaker and H), only one of which is the right one (the speaker).

(13) a. *¿Dónde andan tus hijos?*
      b. *Mira. Diego fue a jugar fútbol, Rorro fue a la playa y Fernando a las carreras.*
      a. 'So where are your sons?'
      b. 'Well. Diego went to play soccer, Rorro went to the beach, and Fernando to the car races.'
(14) a. *A la H no le queda buena,* b. *a mí me quedó buena.*
      'It doesn't fit H,   it fitted me well.'
      Lit.: 'To H not her fits well, to me me fitted well.'   (O,m,17)

When an NP$_1$ (*la H*) is the focus of contrast, then, there is always an element X (*no le queda buena*) which stands in relation to this NP and participates in the contrastive situation in opposition to another element Y (*me quedó buena*) which stands in relation to an NP$_2$ (*a mí*), the alternative contrasting with NP$_1$. There are, then, at least two contrastive elements in a contrastive sentence (NP$_1$ and X) and if the elements with which they contrast are not explicit in the discourse, the information may be inferred.[16]

Examples (15) and (16) exemplify focus of contrast and lend support to our view that word order and intonation interact to signal meaning:

---

[14] There is obviously at least one other choice, clefting, but this will not be discussed.

[15] This suggests that speakers are more ready to change word order than intonation or, in other words, that speakers may want to avoid certain intonational contours. A similar proposal has been made by Laff and Becker (1978) in a study of the effects of intonation on English syntax.

[16] Bransford and Johnson (1972) have conducted psycholinguistic experiments whose results clearly indicate that humans possess the capacity to infer information beyond that which is transmitted literally. The subjects in their experiments frequently thought that they had heard information that they could only have inferred.

(15)   a. *La señorita me mandaba al pan a mí.*

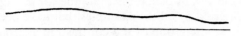

'The lady sent me to buy bread.'
    b. *A las otras no las mandaba.* c. *A mí me mandaba.*

'The others she didn't send. Me she sent.'   (S,f,62)

(16)   [P: talking to I and showing a cut in her finger]
    a. *Tía. Este pasto corta.*
      'Auntie. This grass cuts.'
    [G: responding to P's statement]
    b. *No. A mí no me corta.*

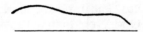

'No. It doesn't cut me.'
Lit.: 'No. To me not me cut.'   (G,f,5)

In (15a) *a mí*, noncontrastive, is postverbal and deaccented. In (15b)–(15c), where a contrast is established between *a las otras* and *a mí*, these Os are preverbal and accented. Example (16b) follows the same pattern. Notice that the information contour is not altered in any of these examples, except for the minor modification added by the deaccented tail in (15a), comparable to the prehead referred to in Section 2.

The fact that the contrastive NP is usually placed in initial position may indicate that it is treated as somewhat old information. Indeed, even when the NP introduces a new referent, the contrastive situation allows the speaker to construct a bridge (Prince, 1978) between this referent and the referent of the NP that it is being contrasted with because both NPs belong to the same specific semantic field, that is, they share some meaning.[17] Thus, the second contrastive NP is interpreted as old, or older, information as

---

[17] More recently, Prince (1981b) has proposed a taxonomy of what she calls "Assumed Familiarity" which includes a three point subdivision of discourse entities into new, inferrable, and evoked. These subdivisions are further broken down into a total of seven different ways in which a given entity may be related to a discourse with respect to its assumed familiarity. However, Prince insists that given–new appear to be a dichotomy. On the contrary, it seems to me that her discussion of given–new information supports my proposal that this is not a dichotomy but that these values are relative and that discourse entities may be analyzed as more or less given with respect to one another.

Carmen Silva-Corvalán

compared to the elements with respect to which the NPs are being contrasted and which provide new information about the contrastive NPs. This line of argument is supported by all the examples that have been discussed here. An analysis of (17), where one of the contrasting alternatives is not explicit but may be identified in the enlarged context, serves to illustrate my point further:

(17) I: a. *¿Y nunca has estado en una situación en que tú digas: '¡Oy! Dios santo ayúdame. Si tú me ayudas yo te voy a rezar', o algo así?*
      o: b. *No. A la Virgen no más le he hecho eso, a la Virgen del Carmen.*
      I: a. And have you ever been in a situation in which you said: "Oh! My God, help me. If you help me I'm going to pray to you," or something like that?
      o: b. No. To the Virgin only I have said that, to Our Lady of Mount Carmel.   (O,m,17)

In (17b) *la Virgen* is contrasted with *Dios.* The implied contrast is that O has made vows to the Virgin but not to God. Note that *la Virgen* is a new referent. However, because it is a focus of contrast and it belongs to the same specific semantic field (divine beings with superhuman powers) as the NP referent that it is being contrasted with (*Dios* 'God'), it is coded as if it were old information and placed in sentence-initial position. The following examples also support this view:

(18) a. (*El papel de nacimiento no lo tengo.*) b. —*Pero carnet tengo.*
      a. '(I don't have my birth certificate.) b. —But my identity card I have.' (S,f,62)
(19) a. *Tengo hartos papeles (para hacer volantines). b. Hilo no tengo.*
      a. 'I have lots of paper (to make kites). b. Thread I don't have.'   (G,f,5)

In (18) and (19), *carnet* and *hilo* are new referents but they are, as predicted, placed in preverbal position and assigned the first point of intonational prominence. Notice, however, that they belong, respectively, to the same specific semantic fields as *papel de nacimiento* and *papeles,* the entities with which they contrast and which have already been mentioned in the discourse. According to my analysis, then, (18b') and (19b'), said with the information contour, are NOT possible alternatives of (18b) and (19b):

(18b') **Pero tengo carnet.*
        'But I have my identity card.'
(19b') **No tengo hilo.*
        'I don't have thread.'

[130]

To summarize, then, the preverbal placement of an O in a sentence with an information contour appears to be reserved for Os that convey older information than the other constituents in the sentence. Between them, word order and intonation signal various functions: relatively high pitch cooccurs with an O that is a center of attention in the discourse, either because it is the discourse topic, a focus of contrast, or a constituent that the speaker intends to highlight for reasons which are demonstrably specific to his discourse plan; relatively low pitch cooccurs with an O that is being used as a discourse link.

The characteristic features of Os with respect to anaphoricity, accent, and sentence position may be compared with those of subject NPs (see Silva-Corvalán, 1982) and thus generalized to all NP constituents as follows: Old information NPs are referred to anaphorically by means of the verb ending in the case of subjects and by means of clitic pronouns in the case of Os.

When the speaker wants to signal an NP as a center of attention, usually because its referent is the discourse topic or a focus of contrast, it will be expressed as a noun or as an independent pronoun and will be assigned the first point of intonational prominence in preverbal position.

Old information subject NPs may be referred to solely by the verb ending in Spanish [Example (20)] or they may be preverbal and accented [Example (21)] or deaccented [Example (22)]. On the other hand, new or newer information subjects are introduced into the discourse in existential constructions with a VS order [Example (23)]. These features and their related functions correspond to what I have shown here about Os. Examples (20)–(23) illustrate the various possibilities for subject NPs:

(20) ZERO SUBJECT:
      Y cuando Ø llegamos ahí Ø ya se habían ido.
      'And when we arrived there they had already left.'
(21) ACCENTED:
      Mi mamá dijo que estaba guapo pero yo no creo. Yo pensaba que estaba feo.
      'My mother said that he was handsome but I don't think so. I thought he was ugly.'
(22) DEACCENTED:
      Así es de que yo hacía el plato y había un negrito que lo cortaba.
      'So I made the plate and there was a black guy who cut it.'
(23) VS:
      Y cuando llegamos a Santa Mónica acá vivían muchos japoneses.
      'And when we came to Santa Monica there lived many Japanese here.'

[131]

In Examples (20) and (22) the subject is old information. It is referred only by the verb ending in (20), in (22) the morphological ambiguity of the verbal form *hacía* motivates its expression.[18] The function of the subject in this type of construction is that of disambiguating its referent. In (22), *yo* is deaccented and might even be left unexpressed. In (21), on the other hand, because *yo* is in contrast with *mi mamá*, it MUST be expressed; it is placed preverbally, and it is said in a relatively high pitch. In Example (23) the subject is introduced for the first time into the discourse and placed in postverbal position.

There seems to be a scale of syntactico-prosodic devices to refer to entities along the old–new continuum which correlate with various functions, as indicated in Figure 1:

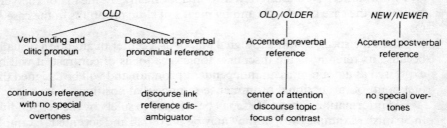

FIGURE 1. Correlation between syntactico-prosodic devices and the old–new continuum.

There are, of course, a number of postverbal possibilities both for Os and for subjects which I have not investigated, as well as two more preverbal object constructions which I shall proceed to discuss.

4. Single Focus Constructions

In this section I discuss a type of OV construction in which the only constituent with intonational prominence is the preverbal object; the rest of the sentence is said on a low level pitch. These constructions are further subdivided into two groups, CONTRARY TO EXPECTATION and FOCAL OBJECTS, according to the motivation for the preverbal placement of the object. The features characteristic of these sentences are compared with those of similar English constructions and shown to be common to both languages.

---

[18] The verbal morphology is the same for first and third person singular in all the tenses of the subjunctive mood, in the imperfect of the indicative, and in the conditional. The verb form alone, then, may ambiguously refer to the speaker or to another participant.

4.1. Contrary to Expectation

In this type of construction an O noun phrase appears in sentence-initial position and is interpreted to be contrary to expectation, that is, there is something surprising about the situation where the O occurs. These OV constructions are different in two respects from the ones discussed in the preceding sections: (*a*) the preverbal O may be new information; and (*b*) the contrary to expectation intonation contour associated with them is different from the information contour.

The contrary to expectation contour consists of an initial peak pitch and an accent with a STEEP fall of the pitch WITHIN THE PREVERBAL OBJECT, the constituents that follow are all deaccented. Examples (24)–(29) are said with the contrary to expectation contour (I have illustrated it in the first two examples only, but the same contour characterizes the rest):

(24)   I: *¿Y tuvieron que pagarle a su–?*
       s: *Ochenta mil pesos dice que le dieron la–* . . .

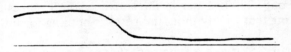

       I: And did they have to pay your–?
       s: Eighty thousand pesos he says they gave him
           the– . . .   (S,f,62)

(25)   R: *¿Y cómo le cortan, le cortan así el pelo, en cualquier parte?*
       F: *Un mechoncito chico pues le sacan no más.*

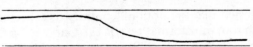

       R: And how do they cut, do they cut the hair, from anywhere?
       F: A small lock of hair they cut him only.   (F,m,70)

(26)   *¡Hasta los calzones los lavaba en el lavaplatos!*
       'Even the underpants she washed in the kitchen sink!'   (S,f,62)

(27)   *Y sentía una pesadez, una pesadez así en la cabeza.—¡Parecía*
       que veinte mil problemas tenía adentro!
       'And I felt a heaviness, a heaviness like this in the head.—It
       seemed as if twenty thousand problems it had inside!'   (R,m,35)

(28)   I: *D tiene cincuenta (años).*
       E: *¡Cincuenta tiene D!*
       I: D is fifty years old.
       E: Fifty D is!   (E,f,34)

(29) F: *Me hicieron seis puntos.*
  I: *¿A sangre fría?*
  F: *A sangre fría. ¡Seis puntos me hicieron!*
  F: They gave me six stitches.
  I: In cold blood?
  F: In cold blood. Six stitches they gave me!   (F,m,70)

In Examples (24)–(27) the DO conveys new/newer information and is expected to occur postverbally. It seems almost natural, and certainly appealing, that in order to convey a surprising situation the elements in a sentence would be placed in an unexpected position, that is, in a new information first rather than the expected old information first order.

In the discourse preceding (24), S has related how one of her sisters and a little child were run over by a car and killed. In her response to the interviewer's question about whether the family had received any compensation, S wants to convey her surprise at the small amount of money they were given (about $2000). Later in the conversation S makes this feeling explicit by saying that 'eighty thousand pesos is nothing for the life of two people.'

The answer in (25) is also a statement that contradicts the questioner's expectation regarding the amount of hair that needs to be cut.[19] Likewise, it is unexpected to have twenty thousand problems inside your head, to be given six stitches without anesthesia, and to wash the underpants in the kitchen sink. The contrary to expectation O is not necessarily new/newer information. Notice that (28) and (29) are repetitions and, therefore, known information.

It has been suggested that the notion "contrary to expectation" plays a role in some English root transformations (RTs) (Gary, 1974; Green, 1980). The preposing of the DOs in (24)–(29) is similar to the effect of the RTs discussed by Gary and some of the inversions discussed by Green, but in Spanish intonation plays a crucial role. Preverbal placement of the O ALONE does not convey contrary to expectation; it must be associated with an intonational configuration: high peak plus steep fall of the pitch on the O, all other constituents deaccented. Furthermore, the distance between the highest and the lowest pitch must be greater than that between these points in the informational contour for the O to be interpreted as contrary to expectation. In fact, intonation also seems to play a crucial role in the corresponding English constructions, as I show later in this section.

[19] F has been explaining that warts may be cured "naturally" by burying some hair from the person who is affected by the warts under a tree next to running water, without the person's being aware of it. R wonders how they are going to cut the person's hair without him noticing it, as if he expected that a lot of hair had to be cut.

4.2. Focal Objects

In focal O constructions the preverbal O conveys the new information. The only structural difference between focal and contrary to expectation Os is the intonation shape associated with them. In both types of constructions the preverbal O is the only accented constituent, but the intonational shape of the focal O itself is that of the information contour, that is, the distance between the highest and the lowest pitch is smaller than in the case of contrary to expectation, and the fall is not steep. I call this intonation shape the FOCAL CONTOUR. Its characteristic is that the two points of prominence (pitch peak and fall) of the information contour fall WITHIN A SINGLE CONSTITUENT and this constituent is followed by a deaccented tail.

Examples (30)–(32) illustrate focal Os:

(30)　I: *¿Pero qué tratamiento le dan a la presión baja, fuera del café con cognac?*

　　　E: *Effortil me dieron a mí.*

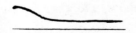

　　　I: So what do they give you for low blood pressure, besides coffee with cognac?

　　　E: Effortil they gave me.　(E,f,34)

(31)　I: *¿Y cuántas inyecciones te pusiste?*

　　　A: *Dos parece que me puse.*

　　　I: And how many shots did they give you?

　　　A: Two it seems to me that they gave me.　(A,f,17)

(32)　I: *¿Cuántos cigarrillos quería?*

　　　M: *Uno no más quería.*

　　　I: How many cigarettes did he want?

　　　M: Just one he wanted.　(M,f,56)

Examples (30)–(32) are question–answer exchanges and the initial O provides the new information requested. The fact that focal Os always convey new information is what differentiates them from all the other OV constructions discussed here. The motivation for the preverbal placement of

[135]

the O in examples like (30)–(32) is not yet clear to me. It is likely that in responses to questions the item that provides the answer may frequently be what first comes to mind. In fact, in many cases the answer consists of only the information requested so that what may need to be explained in focal O constructions is rather the occurrence of the deaccented resumptive information. Obviously this has to be examined systematically in a more comprehensive study of question–answer exchanges.

It is interesting to compare the structure and pragmatic value of single focus constructions [Examples (24)–(32)] with similar constructions in English. An analysis of the English counterparts has been carried out by Prince (1981a), who differentiates between focus movement (FM) and Yiddish movement (YM)[20] constructions on the basis of distribution, discourse function, and dialectal considerations.

The analysis of the examples of YM indicates that they correspond to the cases of contrary to expectation in Spanish. Consider Examples (33) and (34) [Prince's examples (42b) and (43a), respectively]:

(33)   EFP: *What did she see in him?* (*him* = the Scarsdale diet doctor)
        FCC: *Eleven million! ELEVEN MILLION he made, on the Scarsdale diet!*
(34)   Q: *How's your son?*
        A: *Don't ask! A sportscar he wants!*

As in Spanish contrary to expectation constructions, the preverbal O in YM may be old or new information and it is associated with an emphatic falling intonation contour (Prince, 1981a:14).[21] Furthermore, it seems to me that, as in the Spanish examples, the O may be interpreted as contrary to expectation or surprising. This observation is confirmed by Bolinger (p.c.), who points out that the contrary to expectation contour occurs in English in constructions where the beginning of the utterance reflects high emotional impact [Examples (35) and (36) are Bolinger's]:

(35)   *A thousand dollars that dumb mistake cost me.*
(36)   *Why on earth didn't you pay attention to what you were doing?*

[20] Prince uses these terms simply as convenient labels which should not be interpreted as endorsing a transformational analysis. She also examines "topicalizations," which roughly correspond to the OV constructions that I discuss in Sections 2 and 3. In addition, but within a framework of formal analysis, Contreras (1976:89–102) has studied the types of constructions included in Section 4 as cases of "emphatic order" and has proposed that they derive from an optional rule of "theme postposing." In his monograph Contreras does not investigate the pragmatic function of word order in Spanish.

[21] Prince does not explicitly define the "emphatic falling contour" but it may be what I describe as "contrary to expectation."

Examples like (35) point at the possibility that YM may be a feature of a wider ranger of English dialects than Prince assumes. Thus, the dialectal basis for the differentiation into FM and YM is weakened. Rather, the difference appears to be established by the same features discussed for Spanish: intonation, the informational status (old or new) of the O, and the discourse function.

By the same token, English FM constructions correspond to focal Os in Spanish, that is to say, the preverbal O is new information and is assigned final sentence accent. Observe Examples (37) and (38):

(37)   *They just bought a cat. Lady they named it.*
(38)   *Every Sunday I stayed home and read. Two books I read each Sunday.*

Even further, a comparison between (34) and (37), for example, shows that, following Prince's analysis, the only difference between YM with a new information preverbal O and FM is the intonational shape. This is in fact the same difference that I have found between contrary to expectation and focal O constructions.

It is interesting, then, that at least with respect to single focus constructions, there are more similarities than expected between English and Spanish word order. It appears that the differences between these two languages are related only to the behavior of subjects and IOs. First, the obligatory expression of a grammatical subject in English does not seem to permit the same degree of intonational integration of the preverbal O with the rest of the sentence as in Spanish, while it also determines the use of a dummy subject *there* in presentational sentences of the type illustrated in (23). Second, subjects and IOs are relatively more movable in Spanish: they may be placed in preverbal or postverbal position without encoding their referents in a different grammatical relation, for example by means of a passive construction. This explains the higher frequency of use of passive constructions in English and the existence in this language but not in Spanish of IO passivization.

5. Conclusions

I have discussed various types of constructions with a sentence-initial object and shown that this ordering has intonational correlates. Three contours have been identified: the information contour, the contrary to expectation contour, and the focal contour. The data analyzed here have some interesting implications both for discourse – syntax theory and intonation theory.

[137]

It has been shown that there exist certain intonational contours, all of them with a falling shape and with variable pitch heights in initial position, which indicate the role that a preverbal object plays in a discourse. This is evidence that pitch height is meaningful as the same syntactic structure, OVX,[22] may convey different meanings depending on the pitch height assigned to the O or the distance between the highest and the lowest pitch assigned to it. This result unquestionably supports Bolinger's (1972:644) statement that "the distribution of sentence accents is not determined by syntactic structure but by semantic and emotional highlighting." On the other hand, although I have used the term "intonational contour" as if this were a unit of intonation, I do not mean to claim that the analysis supports a holistic model of intonation (as proposed by Liberman and Sag, 1974). It may be possible to break down the contours into sequences of discrete pitches for the purposes of a phonological analysis and at the same time also possible that different meanings may be conveyed by the same contours in situations which have not been investigated in this paper.[23] The analysis presented here has contributed, however, to the establishment for Spanish of an INTONATIONAL LEXICON (Liberman, 1978); that is, I have proposed a small inventory of meaningful contours which contrast with one another, albeit in a very specific structural context: short sentences with a maximum of two accent peaks.

The results of this investigation throw some doubts upon the one-to-one correlation between form and function at the level of syntax. We have seen that the same structural form, OVX, may have different pragmatic functions derived from the preverbal position of the O: discourse link, center of attention, focus of contrast, contrary to expectation. On the other hand, the same structural form may have different intonations that correlate with the different functions. Thus, it seems to me that an account of the relations between syntax and discourse function or meaning must incorporate intonation. Taking the interaction of these two formal levels into account may allow us to give a more adequate explanation of the relation between form, function, and speaker's communicative purposes. It is this relation that I have attempted to capture in the following summary:

1. When a sentence-initial O is old/older information and is assigned the first accent of the INFORMATION CONTOUR we infer that its referent is a

---

[22] As pointed out in Note 20 these OVX constructions have been proposed to correspond to different syntactic structures which reflect the different transformations that generate them: "topicalization" for the OV constructions discussed in Sections 2 and 3, and "theme postposing" or YM and FM for those discussed in Sections 4.1 and 4.2. However, I have shown that the only difference between YM and FM is semantico-pragmatic and intonational and, on the other hand, that topicalizations are associated with different pitch heights on the initial object.

[23] For enlightening reviews of different approaches to the analysis of intonation, see Ladd (1980) and Quilis (1975).

CENTER OF ATTENTION in the discourse because it is either a FOCUS OF CONTRAST, or the TOPIC of a discourse passage, or an IMPORTANT ENTITY[24] in the discourse. If the initial O is not accented we interpret it to be a DISCOURSE LINK.

2. When an initial O is the only sentence constituent with intonational prominence we infer that its referent is CONTRARY TO EXPECTATION or surprising if it is associated with the CONTRARY TO EXPECTATION CONTOUR, or that it conveys the NEW INFORMATION in the sentence if it is associated with the FOCAL CONTOUR.

Acknowledgments

This paper is a thoroughly revised and enlarged version of Chapter 5 of my doctoral dissertation. In its various stages of revision it has benefited from valuable comments and criticism from D. Bolinger, E. García, R. Kirsner, D. R. Ladd, Jr., R. Stockwell, S. Thompson, and B. Wald. I wish to express my gratitude to each one of them. Errors of fact and interpretation are my responsibility.

References

Barrutia, R., and Terrell, T. 1982. *Fonética y fonología españolas*. New York: Wiley.
Bolinger, D. 1954. English prosodic stress and Spanish sentence order. *Hispania* 37, 152–156.
Bolinger, D. 1954–1955. Meaningful word order in Spanish. *Boletín de Filología VII* (Universidad de Chile) 7, 45–56.
Bolinger, D. 1972. Accent is predictable (if you're a mind reader). *Language* 48, 633–644.
Boyce, S., and Menn, L. 1979. Peaks vary, endpoints don't: implications for intonation theory. *Proceedings of the Fifth Annual Meeting of the Berkeley Linguistics Society*, pp. 373–384.
Bransford, J., and Johnson, M. 1972. Contextual prerequisites for understanding: some investigations for comprehension and recall. *Journal of Verbal Learning and Verbal Behavior* 11, 717–726.
Chafe, W. 1976. Givenness, contrastiveness, definiteness, subjects, topics and point of view. In C. Li (Ed.), *Subject and topic*. New York: Academic Press.
Contreras, H. 1976. *A theory of word order with special reference to Spanish*. Amsterdam: North-Holland.
Duranti, A., and Ochs, E. 1979. Left-dislocation in Italian conversation. In T. Givón (Ed.), *Syntax and semantics, vol. 12*. Discourse and syntax New York: Academic Press.
Firbas, J. 1962. Notes on the function of the sentence in the act of communication. *Sborník Prací Filosofické Fakulty Brněnské University* A10, 133–147.

---

[24] I am unhappy about having to use the expression "important entity" because I am unable at this point to provide a context-independent definition for it. A given entity may be identified as "important" in a discourse, however, when it is assigned intonational prominence in spite of being old information.

Gary, N. 1974. *Discourse function of some root transformations.* Distributed through the Indiana University Linguistics Club, Bloomington, Indiana.

Givón, T. 1976. Topic, pronoun and grammatical agreement. In C. Li (Ed.), *Subject and topic.* New York: Academic Press.

Green, G. 1980. Some wherefores of English inversions. *Language* 56, 568–601.

Hatcher, A. 1956. Theme and underlying question: two studies of Spanish word order. *Word* 12. (Monograph No. 3)

Hawkinson, A., and Hyman, L. 1975. Hierarchies of natural topic in Shona. *Studies in African Linguistics* 5, 147–170.

Hyman, L., and Zimmer, K. 1976. Embedded topic in French. In C. Li (Ed.), *Subject and topic.* New York: Academic Press.

Keenan, E. O., and Schieffelin, B. 1976. Topic as a discourse notion: a study of topic in the conversations of children and adults. In C. Li (Ed.), *Subject and topic.* New York: Academic Press.

Ladd, D. R., Jr., 1980. *The structure of intonational meaning.* Bloomington: Indiana University Press.

Laff, M. O., and Becker, L. 1978. The effects of intonation on syntax. Paper presented at the Summer Meeting of the Linguistic Society of America. Urbana, Illinois, 1978.

Li, C., and Thompson, S. 1976. Subject and topic: a new typology of language. In C. Li (Ed.), *Subject and topic.* New York: Academic Press.

Liberman, M. 1978. *The intonational system of English.* Doctoral Dissertation, MIT. (Available through Indiana University Linguistics Club, Bloomington, Indiana.)

Liberman, M., and Sag, I. 1974. Prosodic form and discourse function. In *Papers from the Tenth Regional Meeting of the Chicago Linguistic Society,* 416–427:

Navarro, T. 1966. *Manual de entonación española* (3rd ed.). México: Colección Málaga.

Prince, E. 1978. A comparison of Wh-clefts and It-clefts in discourse. *Language* 54, 883–906.

Prince, E. 1981a. Topicalization, focus-movement, and Yiddish-movement: a pragmatic differentiation. *Proceedings of the Seventh Annual Meeting of the Berkeley Linguistics Society,* 249–264.

Prince, E. 1981b. Toward a taxonomy of given–new information. In P. Cole (Ed.), *Radical pragmatics.* New York: Academic Press.

Quilis, A. 1975. Las unidades de entonación. *Revista Española de Lingüística* 5, 261–280.

Silva-Corvalán, C. 1979. *An investigation of phonological and syntactic variation in spoken Chilean Spanish.* Doctoral Dissertation, University of California, Los Angeles. University Microfilms.

Silva-Corvalán, C. 1981. The diffusion of object–verb agreement in Spanish. *Papers in Romance,* Supplement 2, Vol. 3, 163–176.

Silva-Corvalán, C. 1982. Subject variation in Mexican-American Spanish. In J. Amastae and L. Elías-Olivares (Eds.), *Spanish in the United States: sociolinguistic aspects.* New York: Cambridge University Press.

Wald, B. 1976. *The discourse unit: a study in the segmentation and form of spoken discourse.* Unpublished Manuscript, University of California, Los Angeles.

Wierzbicka, A. 1975. Topic, focus, and deep structure. *Papers in Linguistics* 8, 59–87.

Zubin, D. 1979. Discourse function of morphology: the focus system of German. In T. Givón (Ed.), *Syntax and semantics, vol. 12: discourse and syntax.* New York: Academic Press.

CHAPTER EIGHT

Context Dependence of Language and of Linguistic Analysis

Erica C. García

> *. . . sounds are too volatile and subtile for legal restraints:*
> *to enchain syllables and to lash the wind,*
> *are equally the undertakings of pride,*
> *unwilling to measure its desires by its strength.*
> Dr. Johnson

1. Introduction

Almost any two linguists are likely to agree that discourse is somehow relevant to linguistic analysis; they are even more likely, however, to disagree on the exact nature of the HOW. This is hardly surprising, given that the study of syntax has traditionally viewed the sentence as the unit exemplifying all processes relevant to meaning construal (Bloomfield, 1933:170; Martinet, 1965:223; Lyons, 1968:168). From this point of view, discourse would be no more than a sum, an (unstructured) aggregate of sentences. The recent interest in text or discourse grammars has unquestionably arisen in reaction to that older view of syntax (Hendricks, 1972; Venneman, 1975:314, 323–326; van Dijk, 1977:39–40, 45; and Wolfson, 1979:180 181 are a very small sampling of the relevant literature). In particular, the distribution of pronouns was one of the first problems to resist statement in terms of strictly sentence-bound rules (Lasnik, 1976; Chomsky, 1976:104, 1977:165–166, 182–183; Williams, 1977; Wasow, 1979:147; Evans, 1980:349; Hirst, 1981:85).

But perhaps an even more basic question needs to be raised: What is, after all, the object of linguistic analysis? The recent emphasis on formalization seems to have deflected attention from a fundamental fact: namely, that in a given context form X, rather than Y, or Z, is used. The question of why this is so cannot be answered with "Because that's what the speaker wanted to say!"—unless it can be shown by virtue of what properties X (rather than Y or Z) appropriately conveys what the speaker wants to say and, furthermore, what the speaker wants to say can be established independently of the presence of X.

It should be noted that the problem of "why X rather than Y, or Z" is inescapable, whether or not the answer takes a semantic form: Even a purely distributional analysis must ultimately account for the fact that X, rather than Y or Z, appears in the given context. To be sure, the definition both of "forms"—of what counts as Xs, Ys, or Zs—and of "context" will be influenced by what type of answer is deemed adequate. This point is taken up in Section 6.

In this paper we will examine how the solution of a problem — perhaps, even the very possibility of solving the problem — depends on whether it is the sentence or discourse that serves as the vantage point from which an analysis is undertaken. The issue is far from purely academic, given that the traditional bias in favor of sentence syntax continues to play an important role in linguistic analysis. For instance, a conscious definition of "core" grammar in terms of the sentence is the hallmark of recent work in generative grammar (Chomsky and Lasnik, 1977; Koster, 1980:225–229; Chomsky, 1980), where the fundamental assumption seems to be that adequate formalization is possible only if the scope of the phenomena to be accounted for is severely restricted. This assumption entails (a) that the categories of analysis will be "sentence bound" in a very real sense; and (b) that it is not only necessary, but also appropriate, to distinguish between "core grammar" and "peripheral" phenomena, with the latter standing to the central core in a rather loose, imperfectly understood relation (Koster, 1978; Chomsky, 1977:174–176, 1980).

An alternative to this division of the data is conceivable: ALL uses of a form might actually exemplify one and the same underlying principle, in which case the differences that loom so large for sentence grammar would merely be reflections of the variety of contexts in which the form is privileged to occur. It is clear that if such an analysis is aimed at, the phenomena to be explained cannot be limited to sentence data, nor can the explanation rely on sentence-inspired analytical categories. A unifying analysis must perforce transcend the boundaries of that unit which imposes the division of the data into core versus peripheral phenomena.

That this is possible, precisely by appealing to discourse (rather than sentence) considerations, will be shown by presenting an analysis that accounts, in a unitary way, for both "normal" and "abnormal" uses of pronouns in Spanish prepositional phrases. After a brief introduction of the relevant forms, we shall outline an analysis that explains the occurrence of the forms as due to a communicatively motivated choice, inspired by the larger context. We shall end by discussing briefly the theoretical implications that follow from such a unitary analysis.

2. The Problem in Traditional Terms

The traditional analysis of Spanish *sí* and *él* is not merely sentence bound: It embodies the sentence-based category par excellence, namely, reflexivity. As every schoolchild used to know, a reflexive is a pronoun that "occurs in the predicate and refers back to the subject": By relying on the subject–predicate dichotomy, reflexivity constitutes a paradigm case of sentence-based syntax.

We now present the traditional analysis, illustrating it with examples of the prescribed use of the forms. The following pronouns occur in prepositional phrases:

			SINGULAR	PLURAL
First person			*mí*	*nosotros*
Second person			*tí*	*vosotros*
Third person	reflexive		*sí*	*sí*
	nonreflexive:	Masculine	*él*	*ellos*
		Feminine	*ella*	*ellas*
		Neuter	*ello*	

(1) *Lo compró para mí.*   'He bought it for me.'
     Lo compró para tí.   'He bought it for you.'
     Lo compró para sí.   'He bought it for himself.'
     Lo compró para él.   'He bought it for him.'
     Lo compró para ella.   'He bought it for her.'
     Lo compré para mí.   'I bought it for myself.'
     Lo compré para tí.   'I bought it for you.'
    Lo compré para sí.   ?'I bought it for itself.'
     Lo compré para él.   'I bought it for him.'
     Lo compré para ella.   'I bought it for her.'

Thus, the third person (personal) pronouns appearing in Spanish prepositional phrases are *sí* (invariable for gender and number), and *él* (*ella, ello, ellos, ellas*), variable for gender and number. The standard, almost unanimously accepted analysis of these forms views *sí* as a reflexive pronoun

(Bello, 1964:107, #282) and *él* either as a nonreflexive pronoun (Alarcos Llorach, 1970:152) or, more commonly, as the unmarked third person pronoun. This coheres perfectly with the standard analysis of clitics: *Se* is generally viewed as a third person reflexive; *le, lo, la, les, los, las* as a third person nonreflexive.

There are, however, two difficulties with this analysis. In the first place, *lo compró para él* is open to two interpretations: *él* may, but need not, be coreferential with the subject (Fernández, 1951:221, no. 116). Although this reflexive use is compatible with an analysis of *él* as an unmarked third person personal pronoun, the question remains why speakers should use *él* to do a job for which they have specialized form, namely, *sí*.

In the second place, and much more seriously, *sí* can be used nonreflexively, that is, to refer to something other than the subject (Bello, 1964:108 #283; Fernández, 1951:221 #116; Barker Davies, 1966), as in the following example:

(2) *Para distinguir las **especies** de hongos entre **sí** es preciso atender en primer lugar al color de las esporas.*
'In order to distinguish between mushroom species (lit., to distinguish mushroom species among each other) it is necessary in the first place to attend to the color of the spores.'

Moreover, there are cases like the following, where *sí* does not refer to any element in its clause, let alone the subject:

(3) *Fernando odiaba a su padre. . . . Y aunque lo odiaba, manifestaba muchos rasgos semejantes con él, no sólo rasgos físicos sino de temperamento. . . . Con los años fue repudiando crecientemente aquella semejanza, y pienso que esa semejanza era una de las principales causas del rencor que de pronto estallaba contra **sí mismo**.* (Sábato: 392)
'Fernando hated his father. . . . And though he hated him, he had many traits in common with him, not only physical attributes but also character traits. . . . As the years went by he increasingly rejected that resemblance, and I think that that very resemblance was one of the chief causes of the rancor that kept breaking out against **himself**.'[1]

Here *sí* does not refer to the subject of the sentence (i.e., to the rancor) but rather to Fernando, the subject of *fue repudiando* 'rejected', which is at a considerable distance from the verb *estallaba* 'broke out' with which the *sí* is

[1] Here and throughout the English glosses are my own.

grouped, and which is not even superordinate to the clause in which the *sí* occurs.[2]

The pronouns fail, then, to occur in the prescribed distribution, as both *sí* and *él* (*ella,* etc.) are used to refer both to the subject and to nonsubjects. The standard analysis of *sí* (and *él*) in terms of reflexivity thus prompts a dichotomy of the data, with some instances of *sí* and *él* being classified as regular, and others as exceptional, or abnormal. No explanation is offered, by any of the grammarians dealing with the problem, as to why the abnormal uses should occur at all, or why they should take the form that they do.[3] Exceptions to a rule are apparently regarded as the norm, or as due simply to the language users' ignorance of their own language. This is not necessarily an untenable position; it seems to be held by Otero (1969), who remarks: "*Consigo,* say, can appear in anyone's speech even if the language requires *con él.* . . . Grammars, especially overcrowded fragments such as Spanish pronominalization, are hard to handle adroitly since they require both exceptional discernment and care [p. 1150]." Apparently, as prescriptivists have frequently pointed out, native speakers do not really know their language. They just use it to talk.

An alternative might be to maintain that *sí* is reflexive, and *él* nonreflexive, "in the grammar," but that the distinction is irrelevant to language use, where the two forms are in free variation as far as reflexivity is concerned. The difficulty with such a hypothesis is that the distribution of *sí* versus *él* is far from random: In some contexts (e.g., "reflexive situations") *sí* clearly outnumbers *él,* whereas in others it is in a clear minority (see García, in preparation b, for a discussion of the implications of this problem for variationist analysis).

There is, of course, another alternative: to admit that the standard analysis is clearly disconfirmed in both directions, and that the reason for the choice between *sí* and *él* cannot be found in the reflexivity of the reference. Once this is admitted, nothing is left but to seek the principle that speakers do follow in their use of these forms, and to do so without any commitment to a priori (sentence-inspired) categories.

[2] Note that this situation is not parallel to the types discussed by Postal (1974:64–66) and Koster (1978:243). The example could be made to fit the standard definition of reflexive by claiming, for instance, that the underlying structure of *el rencor estallaba contra X* 'the rancor broke out against *X*' is something like *X estallaba en rencor contra X* '*X* broke out in rancor against *X*', and that reflexivity is properly defined on deep, rather than surface, structures. But this would be an ad hoc maneuver: There is no reason to suppose that any other aspect of Spanish grammar would be clarified by making such assumptions.

[3] Although *sí* is used in Example (3) in refering to an entity other than the subject of the clause, there are instances of reference to nonsubjects where *sí* is never observed. Thus, a husband coming home after having vainly tried, for the fourth day running, to approach his boss for a raise in salary, will not remark to his wife *De nuevo no pude hablar consigo* 'Again it was impossible to speak with him'. In such a context only *él* is found in the texts, or volunteered by native informants.

3. A Communicative Solution

The first thing to be noted is that *sí* is invariable for gender and number, whereas *él, ella, ellos, ellas* do convey this information:

(4)   a. *María lo compró para sí/ella.*
           'Mary bought it for herself.'
        b. *Pedro lo compró para sí/él.*
           'Peter bought it for himself.'
        c. *Los chicos lo compraron para sí/ellos.*
           'The boys bought it for themselves.'
        d. *Las chicas lo compraron para sí/ellas.*
           'The girls bought it for themselves.'

The second thing to be noted is that *le habló de sí* is open to two interpretations:

(5)   a. 'He (*X*) talked to him (*Y*) about himself (*X*)'
        b. 'He (*X*) talked to him (*Y*) about himself (*Y*)'

whereas three are possible for *le habló de él*:

(6)   a. 'He (*X*) talked to him (*Y*) about himself (*X*)'
        b. 'He (*X*) talked to him (*Y*) about himself (*Y*)'
        c. 'He (*X*) talked to him (*Y*) about him (*Z*)'

Sí is not bound to refer to the subject; it IS, however, bound to refer to something in its context. In Evans's (1980:358) terms, *sí* is referentially dependent; *él*, armed with gender and number information, is not.

Now this distinction is not a very useful one, unless we can specify what *sí* is referentially dependent on: Otherwise we shall be introducing an ad hoc distinction, with neither predictive nor explanatory value.

Following the Form–Content approach (Diver, 1975; García, 1975; Kirsner, 1979), we assume that the communicative tool (language) is constantly shaped and reshaped by users with human talents (and weaknesses), and that therefore both the communicative problems posed and the solutions found for these problems must be understandable on the basis of human abilities and deficiencies.

What, then, is the communicative problem behind the use of *sí* and *él* — more generally, what is going on when third person pronouns are used? The fact that reference to something is NOT made via the lexicon forces the hearer to search for — to think of — the referent (Clark and Sengul, 1979:35). But this very fact — that reference is made not via the lexicon — suggests that the lexicon is not absolutely necessary: The referent should be identifiable on other grounds. That is, the hearer is alerted that he will have to, but also should be able to, identify the referent without lexical help (cf. Bolinger, 1979:290, 308).

Notice now that discourse does something extremely important toward the solution of this problem: It provides a context that is expected to be communicatively effective. This effectiveness is due, at least in part, to relations of hierarchy, more central versus less central, etc., among the various entities involved (Clark and Clark, 1977:170–172; Hirst, 1981; Karmiloff-Smith, 1981; Linde, 1979:347; Perfetti and Lesgold, 1977:149). The result of this is that third persons can be expected not to be all on a par, that is, the third persons referred to in the discourse can be expected to differ in degree of salience. In other words, at any given moment the attention of the speech partners will be fixed on one rather than on another third person.

How can differential salience be turned to communicative advantage? Because a host of nonspeakers–nonhearers qualify as third persons, it stands to reason that any property distinguishing among them — even a noninherent, context-dependent property — may be seized on to facilitate the identification of a particular third person. One such property, paradoxically, may be the very difficulty of the search, that is, the varying ease with which the referent can be identified. It is precisely because third persons appear in connected discourse — which guarantees differential salience — that a search in these terms is possible.

Recall that of the two third-person forms we are comparing, one, *si*, is totally devoid of information as to gender and number of its referent, whereas the other, *él*, does carry such information. Nothing could be more sensible, then, than to use *él* where its greater precision is needed, and to reserve *si* for those situations where information as to gender and number can be done without.[4] The natural use of *si* would thus be to refer to a third person that does not need to be sought for or distinguished from others. For a third person — by definition not given by the speech situation itself — this can only be the case when he/she/it positively leaps to mind because he/she/it already is on one's mind (Chafe, 1974:112). It should be clear that at any given point in the discourse there can be only one third person that most eminently satisfies these conditions, and can thus be selected by *si* from among all third persons. It should also be clear that as the discourse proceeds different third persons may successively qualify as candidates for reference by *si*, just as in a conversation different individuals successively qualify for reference by 'I'.

It is because the very coherence of discourse forces a differentiation as to salience among third persons that *si* is dependent on a context-guaranteed

---

[4] See Dahl and Gundel, 1982, for a discussion of focused versus nonfocused pronouns in essentially the same terms.

referent. As for *él*, as already pointed out, the gender and number information it conveys makes it a suitable tool for referents that are less present to the mind. Our hypothesis, then, is that

sí = THIRD PERSON

Because the meaning of *sí* is so extremely poor, it can only be used to refer to what the speaker regards as an extremely obvious third person, about whose identity there can be no doubt; when the addressee hears *sí* used he concludes, in turn, that reference is to the nonspeaker-nonhearer he already has in mind. On the other hand,

él = DEICTIC, with GENDER and NUMBER specifications[5]

Because the meaning of *él* is richer in information than that of *sí*, it can be used to single out one among a variety of third persons that are of comparable salience and/or are not obviously on the mind: The hearer knows, when he hears *él*, that the referent intended must be compatible with the gender and number specified.

It will be useful briefly to point out exactly how our analysis differs from the traditional one. First, and most obviously, it differs in the choice of categories: The traditional analysis regards both *sí* and *él* as third person personal pronouns, differing only in that *sí* is marked for use under the specific and well-defined condition of reflexive reference; our analysis, on the contrary, establishes no common semantic substance between *sí* and *él*.[6] Both may, of course, be used to refer to nonspeakers-nonhearers, but they do so from different perspectives: *Sí* does so as a personal pronoun, the hallmark of these forms being the situational givenness of their referents; *él*, on the other hand, as all deictics, serves to distinguish one given referent from among many.

Second, our choice of analytical categories rests not only on the observed properties of *sí* and *él* (gender information, reference potential) but also on

---

[5] Our analysis of *sí* and *él* is obviously incomplete, but as we are opposing these two forms we give only the traits needed to distinguish between them. *Sí* is also opposed to *se* (clitic) and *su* (possessive); as for *él*, its characterization as a deictic demands a study of its relation to "demonstratives" such as *ése, éste,* and *aquél.*

[6] This analysis differs from the one presented in García (1975:186–193) in the direction of increased motivation by the fundamental communicative problem, and better fit with the data. The difference between the two analyses is discussed in García (in preparation a). By "deictic" we mean only the following:

   (i) That *él* is not a personal pronoun (cf. Benveniste, 1966, for an insightful discussion of "grammatical person")

   (ii) That it selects or points out its referent at least, and perhaps only, via its gender and number information

The fundamental point is that the opposition of (third person) *sí* to (first person) *mí* is different from the "potential equivalents" relation that holds between *sí* and *él*.

general considerations concerning communication (nature of discourse, lexical versus nonlexical reference), which may plausibly be assumed ultimately to shape language itself. It is this kind of motivation that is totally absent from the traditional analysis: No reason is ever given as to why such a category as reflexivity should be useful in the analysis of linguistic phenomena.

Third, and perhaps most important, our analysis of *sí* and *él* does not leave "third person" or "deixis" uninterpreted. These categories are related to the communicative problem at issue via predictions as to the most plausible exploitation of the forms. After all, an abstract meaning, isolated from what speakers are likely to do with it, has very little explanatory value. A Form–Content analyst is not only responsible for the forms and meanings of linguistic signs, but should also demonstrate that a plausible inferential connection links language and language use (cf. Kirsner, this volume). To be sure, the connection suggested between the meanings of *sí* and *él* and the uses to which they are likely to be put may seem painfully obvious. That, however, does not make the link circular. Once the problem is posed in the terms in which we have posed it, the solution may well appear self-evident — but then, the problem has heretofore never been posed in these terms.

4. On Validation

4.1. *Quantitative Validation*

How can an analysis of this type, relying on so obviously subjective a concept as that of "most salient third person," be validated, or, for that matter, invalidated?

In theory we might proceed by taking examples (in context) and showing that replacement of *sí* by *él* always results in reference to a remoter third person and, conversely, that replacement of *él* by *sí* always yields a closer referent. This will not do because in the majority of cases, substitution of *él* for *sí* results in the same individual being referred to, and replacement of *él* by *sí* results in nothing at all.[7]

We might then consider the fact that from the statistical point of view the distribution of *sí* versus *él* appears to be anything but random. Support for our analysis might thus be sought in quantitative data,[8] on the simple-

---

[7] Why this should be so, and why some nonsubjects but not others (cf. Note 3) can be referred to by means of *sí* is taken up in García (in preparation a).

[8] For a discussion of quantitative validation exemplified by data on the use of *le* versus *lo,* see García (1975) and García and Otheguy (1977). Diver (1969), Reid (1977), and Kirsner (this volume) contain valuable discussions of quantitative validation within the Form–Content framework.

minded (but still plausible) assumption that speakers will tend to suit their linguistic means to the problem to be solved, and that more obvious third persons will indeed be referred to with *sí* to a greater extent than less obvious third persons. What this requires, of course, is a characterization of "more" and "less" obvious that is INDEPENDENT of the use of *sí* and *él*. Specifically, we need a parameter on the basis of which it can be predicted, in view of the meaning of *sí* versus *él*, when *sí* will be more appropriate.

Such a quantitative validation of the analysis presented here is certainly possible. For example, the hypothesis advanced allows us to understand why *sí* (rather than *él*) should be used so very frequently to refer to the subject of the sentence. What is usually called "subject" is, after all, the participant in focus (García, 1975:69). The verb ending informs the hearer that the speaker is focusing on an entity with such and such person and number specifications. If anybody or anything can be expected to be present at the center of the hearer's consciousness, this is it (Ertel, 1977:146). Thus *sí* refers so much more frequently than *él* to the subject of its clause not because *sí* is a "reflexive" pronoun but rather because, meaning only THIRD PERSON, it can refer only to an entity which, by being already focused on (being the subject), has become as obvious and self-evident as are the first and the second person. And, indeed, if we compare the relative use of *sí* and *él* to refer to subjects versus nonsubjects, we find a difference of the order of 80% *sí* in references to subjects versus less than 5% *sí* in references to nonsubjects (García in preparation a).

Inasmuch as this skewing coincides with the traditional analysis (which it undoubtedly also motivates) it would be desirable to find some sort of contextual obviousness that is independent of subjecthood. Such test cases are in fact not hard to find. (A preliminary report on distributional skewings appears in García, 1982; García, in preparation a, will contain a thorough quantitative validation of the analysis presented in Section 3.)

We may concentrate, for instance, on reference to the human subject of a sentence, and ask: does it make any difference to the choice of pronoun whether the sentence also mentions a human object or whether the subject is the only human participating in the event? The reference evidently does not cease to be reflexive because a human object happens to be mentioned in addition to the subject; but the prominence and self-evidence of the human subject can certainly be expected to decrease when a human object competes for attention.

Under the standard reflexivity analysis, then, we should expect no difference in the percentage of *sí* whether the sentence contains a human object or not. Our analysis, on the contrary, leads one to expect that the percentage of *sí* will be higher in the absence of a human object, that is, when the subject is the only human involved in the event. A strong skewing in the predicted direction is indeed observable (García, in preparation a), and supports the proposed analysis over the standard reflexivity one.

Further quantitative evidence can be adduced. As pointed out in Section 2, *sí* occurs in prepositional phrases. The prepositional phrase is necessarily grouped with something — for instance, the characterization of an entity. Consider the following constructions:

(7)   a. *Juan compró un libro* [*interesante en* Pro = *libro*]
         'John bought a book   [interesting in itself]'
      b. *Juan compró un libro* [*interesante para* Pro = *Juan*]
         'John bought a book   [interesting for him]'

Though the grouping of the prepositional phrase remains constant, the reference of the pronoun shifts: In (7a) it is to the entity characterized as interesting (i.e., the book); in (7b) it is to John, the subject of the sentence.

Now the traditional analysis should lead us to expect *sí* in examples of type (7b), since reference is from within the predicate to the subject of the sentence, and *él* in the case of (7a). Our analysis makes the opposite prediction: The immediacy of the book in (7a) — guaranteed by the grouping of the prepositional phrase — should enable speakers to make do with *sí*; the diminished salience of the subject in (7b) should *dis*favor *sí*. And, indeed, there is a marked skewing in this direction: In four Argentine authors we find at least 90% *sí* in examples of type (7a), at most 15% *sí* in those of type (7b). There seems thus to be considerable quantitative support for the analysis presented in Section 3.

4.2. Qualitative Validation

That connected discourse constitutes the ideal data base for quantitative validation hardly needs pointing out; it is even more essential, however, to qualitative validation.

The reader will have noted that (*a*) we predict the relative preference for a form, rather than its absolute usage; and (*b*) the skewings observed are not of the "all or nothing" type. The situation confronted, however, is not the familiar case of a traditional rule with exceptions: Rather, we observe statistical norms, with motivated departures therefrom. That the departures from the norm are indeed that, and not counterexamples, must be shown by submitting each departure to meticulous scrutiny. And this scrutiny of individual cases must confirm, rather than disprove, the analysis.

Take an unquestioned skewing: *Sí* is favored when reference is to the (obviously prominent) participant in focus, disfavored when reference is to an entity not mentioned in the clause at all. Nonetheless, there are instances where *sí* is used to refer to such outside referents, just as there are instances where *sí* is avoided and *él* is used instead to refer to the subject of the clause. If our analysis is correct we should expect — and be able to demonstrate — that these are not arbitrary exceptions, but departures from a statistical norm which are motivated by the larger context. It is the context which either makes the "outsider" win out in salience over the subject of the clause or, conversely, detracts from the normal salience of that subject.

Such a demonstration requires a detailed analysis of the context in which — again — INDEPENDENT evidence is sought for the obviousness (or nonobviousness) of the pronoun's referent. To the extent that such independent evidence can be adduced, the departures from the norm will be explained, and will be seen to constitute, not counterexamples, but an invaluable confirmation of the analysis. In this way, qualitative validation controls and complements quantitative validation.

We turn now to a discussion — in context — of instances of pronominal usage which can be viewed either as exceptions to the traditional analyses based on reflexivity, that is, as inherently inexplicable uses of the forms, or, alternatively, as departures from the statistical norm predicted by our analysis. We will seek to show that they should indeed be viewed as locally explainable departures from the norm, the motivation for which they therefore confirm.

We shall examine two types of situations:

1. *Sí* is used to refer to an entity other than the subject of its clause.
2. *Él* is used to refer to the subject.

5. The Data

5.1. Sí *for Nonsubjects*

Our examples are drawn from the works of distinguished Latin American and Spanish writers. As the connection between the particular utterance (clause) being discussed and the larger discourse within which it occurs is critical to our demonstration, summary or discussion of the larger context will be provided as necessary. In doing this we shall perforce be sailing between Scylla and Charybdis: On the one hand, it may be hard to provide an adequate and convincing characterization of the larger context for readers who are unfamiliar with the works from which the examples are drawn, and who therefore have no control over the accuracy of our characterization and interpretation of plot, characters, etc. On the other hand, for those readers who do know the works, what we say will be so self-evident as hardly to deserve stating. We hope for the indulgence of both parties.

We begin with the example from Sábato cited earlier, repeated here for the reader's convenience:

(8)   *Fernando odiaba a su padre. . . . Y aunque lo odiaba,*
        manifestaba muchos rasgos semejantes con él, no sólo rasgos
        físicos sino de temperamento. . . . Con los años fue repudiando
        crecientemente aquella semejanza, y pienso que esa semejanza era
        una de las principales causas del rencor que de pronto estallaba
        contra sí mismo. (Sábato: 392)
        'Fernando hated his father. . . . And though he hated him, he
        had many traits in common with him, not only physical attributes
        but also character traits. . . . As the years went by he increasingly
        rejected that resemblance, and I think that that very resemblance
        was one of the chief causes of the rancor that kept breaking out
        against himself.'

That Fernando is the first person thought of as soon as *sí* tells us that reference is made to neither speaker nor hearer is due to at least two factors:

1. The rancor that broke out is an inanimate entity, and it makes little sense to imagine rancor breaking out against itself: It was more probably directed against some human target — that is, the referent of *sí*.

2. But rancor, by its very nature, also presupposes a person to feel it. The passage mentions two individuals: Fernando and his father, so that in theory the rancor could have been felt by three parties: Fernando/the father/others, and have been directed against the same three entities, yielding a total of nine possibilities. Given the total nonmention of others, and the peripheral involvement of the father, Fernando remains as the prime candidate for the role of rancor experiencer, particularly as it is HIS resemblance to his father that is mentioned as the probable cause of that feeling.

Now, if Fernando is the one feeling the rancor, we must weigh the probabilities of his being periodically angry at himself versus at his father. Given that the passage begins 'Fernando hated his father', and in view of the fact that hate results in permanent, unremitting animosity, whereas the rancor in question kept breaking out, it is most likely that the rancor alluded to is the one Fernando felt against himself, whenever the hateful resemblance forced itself on his attention.[9]

---

[9] The larger context alludes to Fernando's father only incidentally, as the source of what was evil in Fernando's character. Fernando's father never intervenes in the action of the novel, and he does not appear to have been known to the narrator who is here recounting his lifelong acquaintance with Fernando.

[193]

Erica C. García

In this context, then, the intended referent is sufficiently present to the mind to warrant the use of *sí* (meaning only THIRD PERSON).[10] There is still the question why Sábato did not use *él* (*mismo*), since the reference would have been to Fernando just as surely: In this context no other referent makes sense. If there is such a degree of contextual redundancy that it makes no difference what pronoun is used, can it make any difference what form Sábato uses? Most certainly, though the difference is not of the sort that can be conveyed in the gloss of a single sentence.

To appreciate the difference that Sábato's choice of *sí* over *él* does make, let us pose the problem from the vantage point of the writer. Two things can be taken as given from our preceding discussion of this example:

1. The writer wishes to refer to Fernando as the object of intermittently erupting rancor.
2. He knows that the reader's attention is firmly fixed on Fernando: not for nothing is he the (anti)hero of the novel, and the topic under discussion for the last 15 pages.

The writer now has a choice: TO UNDERSCORE THAT PROMINENCE by using a pronoun that relies on the prominence, or to refrain from doing so, by using *él*. In view of Fernando's character (clearly an obsessive type), of the obsessive role played by Fernando in both the heroine's and the narrator's lives, and of the concentration upon Fernando in the particular passage in question, the first choice is clearly the right one, for the simple reason that it is COHERENT with what the author is trying to do, above and beyond the particular message at issue.

In short, we may view the choice of the form as motivated on two levels:

1. At the level of the local communication: Does it solve the particular local problem of referring to Fernando?
2. At the level of the "meta" communication: Does the way in which the local problem is solved reinforce the general coherence of the discourse? (Cf. Silverstein, 1976:34, on the related notion of indexical creativity.)

For the particular use of *sí* we are concerned with in Example (8), this works out as follows:

---

[10] In this example *sí* occurs (as it often does) accompanied by *mismo* 'self'. Since *mismo* conveys the same gender and number information as *él* does it might enable *sí* to "reach" less salient referents, for whose identification gender and number are useful or necessary.

This does not appear to be the case, however. In García (in preparation a) we show that in many contexts *sí mismo* distributes even less like *él* than *sí* does, whereas in others *sí mismo* does parallel *él*. The choice of *mismo* appears, then, to follow independent principles, which is, after all, what we should expect from the fact that it does not commute with *sí* and *él*, but rather combines with them.

[194]

1. *Sí* can be used to refer to Fernando because (in this particular context) Fernando is indeed present to the mind.
2. *Sí* SHOULD be used to refer to Fernando because by relying on Fernando's salience it brings that aspect of Fernando to the fore, thus contributing to the general atmosphere of Fernando-obsession that is characteristic of this part of the novel.

We turn now to an example from Mallea:

(9)   *En el fondo de sí, continuaba en Augusto aquel proceso creciente de desilusión y de cansancio.*   (Mallea: 458)
        'In the depths of himself there continued in Augustus that increase in disillusion and fatigue.'

Again reference is made to the hero of the story, who undoubtedly will be more on the mind of the reader than the actual subject of the sentence (i.e., the increase in disillusion and fatigue). He is furthermore presupposed by that increase: The disillusion and fatigue that keep increasing in him are his. Augustus is thus doubly prominent: As the hero of the story, and as the experiencer (and locus) of the disillusion.

But if Augustus is so prominent, why is it that Mallea did not make him the subject of the sentence to start with, instead of relegating him to a prepositional phrase? The reason for Mallea's apparently rather convoluted choice — that is, to refer to Augustus by means of *sí*, and yet to debar him from focus — becomes clear when we consider the plot of the story, which concerns Augustus's loss of faith in life and in himself. In the paragraph preceding the quotation just given we read:

'Augustus would let the newspaper fall and step to the balcony. . . . He let his gaze wander as if he sought a point on which to think without feeling mortification, released from care, without careworn or disgusted reflexion. A thoughtful man, he scanned with an indefinable sensation of disgust and repugnance the general view of a humanity in which, if one were to judge by so many signs, it no longer paid to take part save in order to deceive, and it seemed to him that behind the very twilight a world lay hidden in which life was almost pointless, a tiring and uninteresting world. . . .'

His wife's efforts to cheer him up are of no avail, although

'their life went on normally as far as social contacts were concerned. They attended theaters and shows, dined with friends, chatted and laughed about serious and trivial events. . . .'

But all this did not help:

[195]

'In the depths of himself there continued in Augustus that increase in disillusion and fatigue.'

If Mallea had made Augustus the subject of the sentence, and had written:

(9) *Augusto seguía sintiendo en el fondo de sí mismo un aumento* . . .
     'Augustus continued to experience in the depths of himself an increase . . .'

he would have been describing what Augustus feels and thinks. The whole point of the story, however, is what happens TO Augustus. Augustus cannot control his loss of faith: It grows on him independently of all he can think, wish, or do. Augustus's helplessness in the face of his increasing disillusion, and the relentlessness of that increase, come across more intensely if presented from a detached, impersonal perspective, which in turn is best conveyed if the increase in disillusion is made the subject of the verb *continuaba* 'continued', and Augustus is debarred from prominence by being relegated to a prepositional phrase. This choice is not only made possible by the larger context; it also contributes to the coherence of the story as a whole.

Our argument, then, is that—congruently with what precedes and follows in the story (Augustus's suicide)—Mallea wished the reader to understand that:

1. Despite Augustus's surface social life, the disillusion continued to grow.
2. It did so in the secret depths of Augustus's soul.
3. Augustus had no control over the process.
4. The depths where the process went on were really the very essence of Augustus.

Such a communication can best be accomplished by equating as much as possible Augustus with (the locus of) the process itself. To this end, *sí* is clearly more appropriate than *él*, since being by nature incapable of suggesting new referents, *sí* helps to keep (the) one and only relevant third person firmly in mind.

The examples discussed so far should contribute to the understanding of the following passage by Gallegos, a distinguished Venezuelan writer:

(10) *Era la luz que él mismo había encendido en el alma de Marisela, la claridad de la intuición en la inteligencia desbastada por él . . . la obra—su verdadera obra, porque la suya no podía ser exterminar el mal a sangre y fuego, sino descubrir, aquí y allá, las fuentes ocultas de la bondad de su tierra y de su gente—su obra, inconclusa y abandonada en un momento de despecho, que*

> *le devolvía el bien recibido, restituyéndolo a la estimación de sí*
> *mismo. . . .*
> 'It was the light which he himself had lit in the soul of Marisela,
> the clarity of intuition in the intelligence he had
> quickened . . . the work—his true work, because his task could
> not be the destruction of evil by blood and fire, but rather the
> uncovering, here and there, of the secret springs of good in his
> land and in his people—his work, unfinished and abandoned in
> a moment of resentment, which now returned to him the good
> [it had] received, restoring him to the esteem of himself.'

Santos Luzardo (the person referred to as *él* 'he') is the obvious candidate for reference by this *sí*: because in this particular passage only two people are involved (Marisela and himself), because this chapter deals with his spiritual crisis after a killing, and because he is the hero of the novel.[11] Note, moreover, that the sentence where the *sí* appears can be reduced to

(11)   *su obra le devolvía el bien recibido, restituyéndolo a la estimación*
        de sí mismo
        'his work returned to him the good [it had] received, restoring
        him to the esteem of himself'

Here Santos Luzardo alone is involved, and he is referred to three times (by means of *su*, *le*, and *lo*) before the final *sí*. He is not the subject of the sentence, but he is unquestionably present to the mind of the reader.

Once again we must ask over what alternatives Gallegos chose the observed formulation. The first alternative to be considered is a personal construction instead of a nominalization. Gallegos might have written, for instance

(11')   *su obra le devolvía el bien recibido, permitiéndole estimarse a sí*
        mismo
        'his work (i.e., Marisela, who had benefited from his civilizing
        labors) returned to him the good (it had) received, thus enabling
        him to esteem himself'

This alternative destroys the original parallelism between *devolver* 'return' and *restituir* 'restore'. Note moreover that in Gallegos's formulation these two events contrast in a curious shift in role for the hero: Where his past good actions are spoken of, Santos Luzardo is cast as a recipient, in the dative (*le*). But where *esteem* is involved, he is assigned a totally passive role

---

[11] Another, very important, reason for Santos Luzardo's holding the reader's attention throughout the passage is that the story is told from his, rather than Marisela's, point of view (see Shopen, 1972: 347–348).

(*lo*). Why this shift, and how does it relate to Gallegos' choice of the nominal construction *estima de sí mismo*?

The explanation emerges when we consider the larger context, which in this case spans the entire novel. Santos Luzardo attempts to regain his patrimony and to save it from the backwardness and lawlessness symbolized by Doña Bárbara; one of his good deeds has been the rescue of his cousin Marisela. But the struggle with barbarism is so hard that in a moment of weakness he yields to the temptation of fighting violence with violence, and a man is killed. Santos Luzardo, tormented by remorse, is about to despair, when Marisela draws his attention to a detail he had overlooked, and which conclusively proves that the fatal bullet cannot have been his. He is thereby restored to his original faith in himself.

Santos Luzardo's problem, then, is that he feels that he has failed his own ideals of decency, and is thus unworthy of esteem: his own, and that of others. Since Santos Luzardo sees himself as marked by the killing, with esteem standing for those higher principles he is afraid to have failed, he must be restored to it, rather than having esteem return to him. But this passive role of Santos Luzardo with respect to esteem makes a formulation such as

> *permitiéndole estimarse a sí mismo*
> 'enabling him to esteem himself'

quite inappropriate. The personal construction (or the use of *él* with the nominalization) suggests an active role for Santos Luzardo, thus missing the essential point, namely, that Santos Luzardo cares about being worthy of esteem, that values and ideals have objective reality for him. It is only when he realizes that esteem of himself is possible at all that Santos Luzardo comes to regain a feeling of esteem for himself: With respect to *estima* both the "experiencer" role and the more essential "object" role are conveyed and conflated, in pregnant imprecision, by *de sí mismo*.

We turn, finally, to what may be regarded as a real tour de force in exploiting the value of *sí*, namely Garcilaso's use of this form in his Copla III. Our choice of this example is motivated by its extremely "abnormal" character, both from the point of view of the standard analysis, and in terms of (in)frequency. The fact that the example dates from the sixteenth century does not detract from its relevance: It was as abnormal then as it is now, to judge by the examples Gessner (1893: 15) gives of *sí* used where *él* would be expected by the reflexivity analysis. Conversely, this boldness of usage might well be resorted to by a modern poet.

(12)   *Yo dejaré desde aquí*
        De ofenderos más hablando,

Porque mi morir callando
Os ha de hablar por mí

Gran ofensa os tengo hecha
Hasta aquí en haber hablado,
Pues en cosa os he enojado
Que tan poco me aprovecha.

Derramaré desde aquí
Mis lágrimas no hablando,
Porque quien muere callando
Tiene quien hable por sí.   (Garcilaso: Copla III)

'I shall henceforth
Cease to offend you by speaking,
Because my death in silence
Shall speak to you in my behalf.

I have greatly offended you
Hitherto in having spoken,
Since I have angered you
In what avails me so little.

Henceforth I shall shed
My tears saying nothing,
Because he who dies in silence
Has (someone, i.e., his own death) who will speak for **himself.**'

This example is clearly irreconcilable with the standard definition of reflexivity, but its "ungrammaticality" is matched only by the clarity, appropriateness, and force of *sí*, which refers to the poet (= *quien muere callando* '(he) who dies in silence') out of a tensed clause (*hable* 'will speak') with a different subject, namely, death. The referent of *sí* is nonetheless unambiguously identifiable at the first reading, because there is no one but the dead poet for whom 'speaking in behalf of' is so obviously relevant. The *sí* is justified also from another perspective: Since what will speak in the poet's behalf is the poet's own death, the poet could well be said, after all, to be speaking for himself. We have here an elegant presentation of a single being under two different guises, and/or a blending of two discrete entities into a single event. The alternative views — the poet has died, but his death will make him live in his lady's mind — constitute a paradox that is at once posed and solved by means of the synthesizing *sí*. Here too, as in the examples discussed previously, the use of *sí* is motivated by the self-evidence of the pronoun's referent, and indirectly contributes to enhance that referent's prominence.

[199]

5.2. El *for Subjects*

We have been concerned so far with cases where *sí* refers to some entity other than the subject of the clause in which it appears, and we have seen that in every instance it is not the sentence but the larger context that plays a critical role in making the referent of *sí* the third person present to the mind. We turn now, briefly, to the converse case: *El* is used to refer to the participant in focus, which, all other things being equal, would be expected to be the most prominent entity. The larger context ought to provide the reason(s) why this expectation is not realized in the particular cases. We begin with a particularly telling example:

(13)   *Juan había metido dos dedos . . . dedos que salían de la
       azucarera con un terrón . . . , y en vez de echarlo en su taza
       se acercaban a la taza de Hélène y dejaban caer suavemente el
       terrón, y entonces vi . . . que Hélène miraba a Juan, lo miraba
       de una manera que nadie habría encontrado extraña si no
       hubiera visto al mismo tiempo el gesto de Juan, pero yo sí, yo
       sentí que era otra cosa, una negativa, un rechazo infinito de ese
       gesto de Juan, de ese terrón de azúcar que Juan había echado en
       el café de Hélène, y Juan se dio cuenta porque retiró bruscamente
       la mano y ni siquiera tomó azúcar para él, miró a Hélène un
       instante antes de bajar los ojos, y fue como si de golpe se cansara
       o estuviera ausente o como si se sometiera amargamente a una
       injusticia. Y solamente entonces Hélène dijo: "Gracias".*
       (Cortázar: 142–143)
       '. . . Juan had reached out with his fingers . . . fingers which
       came out of the sugar-bowl with a lump of sugar between them,
       and instead of dropping it in his cup they approached Hélène's
       cup and let the sugar lump fall gently, and then I saw . . . that
       Hélène looked at Juan, she looked at him in a way which
       nobody would have found strange if at the same time they had
       not seen Juan's gesture, but I had, I felt that it was something
       else, a denial, an infinite rejection of that gesture of Juan, of that
       lump of sugar that Juan had dropped into Hélène's coffee, and
       Juan noticed it because he suddenly withdrew his hand and he
       did not even take sugar for himself, he looked at Hélène for an
       instant before dropping his eyes, and it was as if he suddenly
       grew tired or had withdrawn or as if he submitted bitterly to an
       injustice. And only then did Hélène say "Thank you".'

The reader will surmise (correctly) that Juan's unreciprocated love for Hélène is an important element in Cortázar's *62*. Let us consider how it affects the particular event of (not) helping oneself to sugar.

In situations of 'helping to sugar' the participant in focus is normally the most likely candidate to receive the sugar so that, in this case, Juan would be the first one to come to mind as a likely sugar-recipient. However (as is abundantly clear from the context), the story is being recounted from Juan's perspective, and Juan is in love with Hélène. From Juan's point of view it is far more interesting to help Hélène rather than himself to sugar. This is a situation, then, where two third persons (for different reasons) enjoy a comparable degree of prominence: Juan is the participant in focus, on whom the narrator is concentrating; Hélène, on the other hand, is the one Juan is interested in, and who gets the sugar first.

There is thus a double contrast: Hélène, rather than Juan, is helped to sugar in the first place; Juan might (and normally would) have taken sugar for himself, but in view of Hélène's repulse he does not. Juan, then, is by no means the only possible, self-evident third person: Hence the choice of *él* by Cortázar. If *sí* had been used, Juan would have been referred to just as effectually, thought not as effectively, since the contrast, almost the rivalry, between Juan and Hélène would not have been brought out. And it is this contrast that contributes to the tension of the passage, so superbly conveyed in the final sentence.

El can be used not only in situations of contrast between the participant in focus and another (important) entity in the context, as in the example just discussed, but also to suggest a contrast of the participant in focus with himself, a "splitting" of the subject in two, as in the following example:

(14)   *Tampoco hizo mal . . . en ocultar su personalidad y en no mentar su yo . . . porque los poetas épicos y los historiadores, que deben servir de modelo, no dicen yo aunque hablen de **ellos mismos** y ellos mismos sean héroes y actores de los casos que cuentan.* (Valera: 145)
'Neither did he err . . . in concealing his identity and in not alluding to himself . . . because epic poets and historians, whose example we should follow, do not say I though they speak of themselves and are themselves heroes and actors of the events they recount.'

Valera opposes here the two roles played by epic poets and historians: as actors in the events they narrate, and as narrators of the events in which they acted. An attitude of objective detachment is presented as worthy of praise, and this attitude requires that the two roles be dissociated as much as possible. This, in turn, can be achieved by deemphasizing the identity of the two parties. To accomplish this, one of the roles (the actor role which is talked about) must be referred to as it would be if it were distinct (in reference) from the other. This is precisely what *él* does, by suggesting a multiplicity of non-self-evident third persons among which the referent must be identified.

We see, then, that just as in the case of reference to nonsubjects by means of *sí*, the use of *él* to refer to the subject is understandable in the light of the context. For one reason or another, the prominence of the subject is not to be taken for granted; other entities, too, deserve our attention, and the distinguishing force of deictic *él* is therefore appropriate.

6. Discussion

The examples discussed in the preceding section are, of course, merely illustrative. Even if a corpus were to be analyzed in detail, down to the last case of *sí* and *él*, new uses are always possible, in response to as yet unencountered communicative needs, for which the meanings of *sí* and *él* are just as appropriate as they are to the familiar uses. Our interest must lie, consequently, in the value of qualitative validation, and in its relation to the quantitative method briefly described in Section 4.1.

Let us begin by recalling the fundamental problem in linguistic analysis, namely, how to account for the fact that in a given context form X, rather than Y, or Z, is used, or, to put it in distributional terms, how to state the distribution (privilege of occurrence) of form X as opposed to form Y.

The answer we should ideally like to give to this question would no doubt take the form of a statement of complementary distribution (Householder, 1954, 1962): If the forms are different they should, after all, be used differently, and this implies occurrence under different conditions. The sixty thousand dollar question is, of course, in what terms to state the distribution of forms, so that the expected complementarity becomes patent. It is here that the different choices of theoretical perspective can most clearly be seen to bear on the analytical categories resorted to.

A good starting point is the kind of data that underlie our quantitative validation, and probably also motivate the traditional sentence-oriented grammar. Complementary distribution is approximated in such obvious correlations as reference to the subject via *sí* versus reference to a nonsubject via *él*. These facts are statable in the form of a rule couched in absolute, clearly definable terms, which make falsification of the analysis possible. One such formulation might be the following:

(15)   a. If the reference in a prepositional phrase is to a third person subject, use *sí*.

        b. If the reference in a prepositional phrase is to a third person other than the subject, use the form of the *él* paradigm that corresponds to the gender and number of the referent.

If (as in this particular case) the correlation is sufficiently strong, the temptation is likewise very strong to ignore any counterexamples to the rule, as if they were mere exceptions to a rule of morphology. In this way description is mistaken for explanation, and it is assumed that *sí* (rather than *él*) is used in prepositional phrases to refer to a third person subject BECAUSE there is in the language a convention to that effect (whatever that is supposed to mean).

Now the iconoclastic role of qualitative validation becomes clear. If it turns out that the alleged exceptions are explainable by an analysis that also covers the purported convention, then the terms in which the skewed distribution has been put cannot possibly be regarded as the ultimate truth: They can only be particular, more or less frequent manifestations of a more basic, generally valid principle. And, indeed, we have seen that the same rationale that underlies the choice of form for the bulk of cases (those amenable to quantitative statement) likewise explains the departures from the norm. There is an undeniable similarity between the "normal" use of *sí* in (16):

(16)   *Fernando se enfurecía consigo mismo.*
       'Fernando grew furious against himself.'

and Sábato's "abnormal" use of *sí* in the lines from (8), repeated here as (17):

(17)   *esa semejanza era una de las principales causas del rencor que de pronto estallaba contra sí mismo*
       'that resemblance was one of the chief causes of the rancor that kept breaking out against himself'

The similarity is, of course, the equal prominence of Fernando in both situations. Though the reason for the prominence is different (in the one case it lies close at hand, whereas in the other it is diffused through the larger context), the quality of "present to the mind," which justifies the use of *sí*, is the same in both instances. It is this sameness in motivation that is ignored, and implicitly denied, by the division between "grammatical/regular" and "peripheral/abnormal" use forced by the categories of sentence grammar.

Qualitative validation thus puts quantitative correlations in true perspective: *Sí* is certainly used to refer to the subject of a sentence, but it is so AS a rule, never BY a rule. Correlations merely reflect, over a large number of instances, the same phenomenon that is highlighted in the single instance by qualitative validation, namely, a judgment by a user of the language that one meaning is more appropriate than another to a situation characterized by a particular trait.

But qualitative validation has an even more devastating implication. Although in our discussion of the various departures from the norm we kept appealing to the same underlying principle, we also appealed to different (and in principle unpredictable) ad hoc realizations of that principle "in context." The different possible realizations of an underlying principle are thus open ended in number: not only not defined, but in fact not even definable (cf. Hockett, 1968, for fundamentally the same point). Indeed, as context changes (which it must, by its very nature) infinitely many different aspects of events and entities have a chance of being perceived as relevant.

We do not know, a priori, which or how many contextual factors may/will influence the obviousness of a referent, at least not in our present state of ignorance concerning the workings of the human mind. What kinds of referents, under what conditions, are more likely to capture the attention of speaker and/or hearer is a matter for empirical investigation,[12] but there is no reason to suppose that the number or even the type of relevant considerations can be defined a priori. If our knowledge of psychology were better we might, perhaps, be able to describe the process whereby the categorization of various aspects of events and entities takes place, that is, characterize what is meant by "judging a meaning appropriate to a situation." But what PARTIC-ULAR traits will warrant such a judgment cannot be predicted, and certainly not in the absolute terms necessary for formalization.

We must face up to the fact, then, that the ideal of perfect complementary distribution between different forms is attainable, but at a price: The statement thereof cannot be tied to absolute categories of usage, that is, to local manifestations of a general principle. The complementarity resides, ultimately and fundamentally, in the human ability to categorize events and entities as belonging to one "virtual" type as opposed to another. In short, it is the intelligent language user who plausibly (but no more) decides what (in this context) counts as what. Hence the infinite resourcefulness of language; hence, also, misunderstandings, variability, and language change; hence, finally, the inherent impossibility of formalizing an analysis such as ours in absolute terms, and of demonstrating, in a mathematically exhaustive manner, the complementary distribution of *sí* and *él*. Recourse to absolute categories (such as are commonly appealed to in sentence grammars) certainly does result in formal(ized) and hence invalidatable analyses. But these analyses are not merely falsifiable: They are also doomed to invalida-tion, because they purposely bypass the one element behind both the oneness of the use of a form and the complementary distribution of different forms, namely, the judgment and creative imagination of the language user.

---

[12] It is this that must eventually account for the observations alluded to in Note 3.

7. Summary and Conclusions

The analysis of *sí* and *él* proposed in Section 3 can account, in a unified way, for all uses of these forms: not only for those that are readily understandable within the context of the immediate sentence, but for the remainder as well. Our unified analysis is only possible thanks to:

1. The rejection of a familiar categorization in terms of reflexivity, on the grounds that this categorization is incapable of accounting in a coherent way for all of the data
2. The willingness to look afresh at phenomena presumed familiar against the background of discourse

It was this fresh perspective that led us to posit different analytical categories, capable of accounting, in a more satisfactory manner, for all the data.

The (statistical) norm, which traditional grammar interprets as the results of an absolute-type categorization rooted in the logical or propositional structure imputed to the sentence, is, from our perspective, only the natural result of speakers' using the linguistic means at their disposal in the most appropriate manner. In the "abnormal" situations exactly the same is true: Where reference transcends sentence boundaries, *sí* likewise refers to the most salient third person in the context, whereas within the sentence *él* is used to refer to an entity whose prominence is challenged, whether subject or nonsubject. These cases depart from the norm only in that a larger than usual stretch of context provides valid reasons for salience, or detracts from salience (cf. Klein, this volume, for a similar point in relation to position of the adjective).

The type of analysis (and of validation) presented here is certainly not subject to either formalization or strict falsification, as it relies on an in principle open-ended set of (possibly relevant) ill-defined criteria. This, however, does not make the criteria circular, irrelevant, or uncheckable. Nor does it necessarily constitute an indictment of the analysis: The coherence of discourse itself is, by its very nature, open ended, context sensitive, and ill defined. And it is this coherence, after all, that constitutes the ultimate touchstone; for the use of language, just as much as for linguistic analysis.

Acknowledgments

I am indebted to A. Hawkinson, R. S. Kirsner, F. P. Klein, E. Lattey, B. R. Lavandera, R. L. Otheguy, F. van Putte, W. H. Reid, S. Romaine, and Y. Tobin for helpful suggestions and searching criticism of earlier versions of this paper.

References

Alarcos Llorach, E. 1970. *Estudios de gramática funcional del español.* Madrid: Gredos.

Barker Davies, J. 1966. Ajuste sematosintáctico en los pronombres *se, él y sí. El español actual* 8, 4–7.

Bello, A. 1964. *Gramática de la lengua castellana* (7th ed.). Buenos Aires: Sopena.

Benveniste, E. 1966. La nature des pronoms. In *Problèmes de linguistique générale.* Paris: Gallimard.

Bloomfield, L. 1933. *Language.* New York: Holt, Rinehart and Winston.

Bolinger, D. 1979. Pronouns in discourse. In T. Givón, *Syntax and semantics, 12: discourse and syntax.* New York: Academic Press.

Chafe, W. 1974. Language and consciousness. *Language* 50, 111–133.

Chomsky, N. 1976. *Reflections on language.* London: Temple Smith.

Chomsky, N. 1977. *Essays on form and interpretation.* Amsterdam: North-Holland.

Chomsky, N. 1980. On binding. *Linguistic Inquiry* 11, 1–46.

Chomsky, N., and Lasnik, H. 1977. Filters and control. *Linguistic Inquiry* 8, 425–504.

Clark, H., and Clark, E. 1977. *Psychology and language.* New York: Harcourt Brace Jovanovich.

Clark, H., and Sengul, C. J. 1979. In search of referents for nouns and pronouns. *Memory and Cognition* 7, 35–41.

Dahl, D. and Gundel, J. 1982. *Identifying referents for two kinds of pronouns.* Unpublished manuscript. Department of Linguistics, University of Minnesota.

Diver, W. 1969. The system of relevance of the Homeric verb. *Acta Linguistica Hafniensia* 12, 45–68.

Diver, W. 1975. Introduction. *Columbia University Working Papers in Linguistics* 2, 1–26.

Ertel, S. 1977. Where do the subjects of sentences come from? In S. Rosenberg (Ed.), *Sentence production: developments in research and theory.* Hillsdale, N.J.: Erlbaum.

Evans, G. 1980. Pronouns. *Linguistic Inquiry* 11, 337–362.

Fernández, S. 1951. *Gramática española.* Madrid: Revista de Occidente.

García, E. 1975. *The role of theory in linguistic analysis.* Amsterdam: North-Holland.

García, E. 1982. Evidencia del carácter no reflejo de *sí.* In G. Bellini (Ed.), *Actas del VII Congreso de la Asociación Internacional de Hispanistas.* Rome: Bulzoni.

García, E. In prep. a. *Person versus deixis in Spanish prepositional phrases* (provisional title).

García, E. In prep. b. *Shifting variation.*

García, E., and Otheguy, R. 1977. Dialect variation in *leísmo:* a semantic approach. In R. Fasold and R. Shuy (Eds.), *Studies in language variation.* Washington D.C.: Georgetown University Press.

Gessner, E. 1893. Das spanische personal Pronomen. *Zeitschrift für Romanische Philologie* 17, 1–54.

Hendricks, W. O. 1972. Current trends in discourse analysis. In B. B. Kachru and H. F. W. Stahlke (Eds.), *Current trends in stylistics.* Edmonton: Linguistic Research.

Hirst, G. 1981. Discourse-oriented anaphora resolution in natural language understanding: a review. *American Journal of Computational Linguistics* 7, 85–98.

Hockett, C. 1968. *The state of the art.* The Hague: Mouton.

Householder, F. W., Jr. 1954. Review of subjunctive and optative, by A. Hahn. *Language* 30, 389–399.
Householder, F. W., Jr. 1962. On the uniqueness of semantic mapping. *Word* 18, 173–185.
Karmiloff-Smith, A. 1981. The grammatical marking of thematic structure in the development of language production. In W. Deutsch (Ed.), *The child's construction of language*. London: Academic Press.
Kirsner, R. S. 1979. *The problem of presentative sentences in Modern Dutch*. Amsterdam: North-Holland.
Koster, J. 1978. *Locality principles in syntax*. Dordrecht: Foris.
Koster, J. 1980. Configurational grammar. *Gramma* 4, 212–233.
Lasnik, H. 1976. Remarks on coreference. *Linguistic Analysis* 2, 1–22.
Linde, C. 1979. Focus of attention and the choice of pronouns in discourse. In T. Givón (Ed.), *Syntax and semantics, 12: discourse and syntax*. New York: Academic Press.
Lyons, J. 1968. *Introduction to theoretical linguistics*. Cambridge: Cambridge University Press.
Martinet, A. 1965. Réflexions sur la phrase. In *La linguistique synchronique*. Paris: Presses Universitaires de France.
Otero, C. P. 1969. The syntax of mismo. In A. Graur (Ed.), *Actes du X° Congrès International des Linguistes*, vol. II, 1145–1150.
Perfetti, C. A., and Lesgold, A. M. 1977. Discourse comprehension and sources of individual differences. In M. A. Just and P. A. Carpenter (Eds.), *Cognitive processes in comprehension*. Hillsdale, N.J.: Erlbaum.
Postal, P. 1974. *On raising*. Cambridge, Mass.: MIT Press.
Reid, W. H. 1977. The quantitative validation of a grammatical hypothesis: the passé simple and the imparfait. In J. A. Kegl, D. Nash, and A. Zaenen (Eds.), *Proceedings of the seventh annual meeting of the North Eastern Linguistic Society*.
Shopen, T. 1972. Logical equivalence is not semantic equivalence. *Papers from the eighth regional meeting, Chicago Linguistic Society*.
Silverstein, M. 1976. Shifters, linguistic categories, and cultural description. In K. H. Basso and H. A. Selby (Eds.), *Meaning in anthropology*. Albuquerque: University of New Mexico Press.
van Dijk, T. A. 1977. Acceptability in context. In S. Greenbaum (Ed.), *Acceptability in language*. The Hague: Mouton.
Venneman, T. 1975. Topics, sentence accent, ellipsis: a proposal for their formal treatment. In E. Keenan (Ed.), *Formal semantics of natural language*. Cambridge: Cambridge University Press.
Wasow, T. 1979. *Anaphora in generative grammar*. Ghent: Story scientia.
Williams, E. 1977. On "deep and surface anaphora." *Linguistic Inquiry* 8, 692–696.
Wolfson, N. 1979. The conversational historical present alternation. *Language* 55, 168–182.

Sources of Data

Cortázar, J. 1972. *62, modelo para armar* (4th ed.). Buenos Aires: Sudamericana.
Gallegos, R. 1971. *Doña Bárbara*. México: Orión.
Garcilaso de la Vega. 1980. *Poesías completas*. Madrid: Alianza Editorial.
Mallea, E. 1970. *El resentimiento* (2nd ed.). Buenos Aires: Sudamericana.
Sábato, E. 1970. *Sobre héroes y tumbas*. Buenos Aires: Sudamericana.
Valera, J. 1971. *Pepita Jiménez* (11th ed.). Buenos Aires: Losada.

CHAPTER TEN

On the Use of Quantitative Discourse Data to Determine Inferential Mechanisms in Grammar

Robert S. Kirsner

1. Introduction

Most if not all schools of linguistics recognize that the MEANING signaled by a grammatical form (i.e., the information associated with a particular case, tense, particle, etc.) is far more abstract than the multitude of rich, concrete, particular MESSAGES communicated through the use of that form in different linguistic and extralinguistic contexts. The "gap" between abstract meaning and concrete message has profitably been viewed as being bridged through a PROCESS OF INFERENCE — the basic human capacity to solve problems, to leap to conclusions compatible with, but only suggested by, the data given (cf. García, 1975:40–44; Kirsner, 1979:26–31). Accordingly, to fully understand why a particular form has the particular uses that it has (and no others), the grammarian must do two things:

1. Hypothesize a meaning for the form which is capable of explaining the FULL RANGE of messages the form can communicate, without counterexamples or appeals to "idiom"
2. Delineate as explicitly as possible the particular MECHANISM used in bridging the inferential gap between meaning and message.

Until now, the emphasis in most linguistic work (at least that undertaken within Saussurean premises) has lain quite correctly on Task (1), for unless one demonstrates that a proposed meaning is consistent with the total distribution of the form in question, one has, strictly speaking, no analysis. But, for any analysis to be fully convincing, one must go beyond (1) to (2).

Ideally, one should be able to pin down to at least some degree the actual path ("trajectory" might be better) followed from meaning to message and show how that path is both consistent with the meaning hypothesized and in accord with the facts of usage. To the extent that one can actually demonstrate that a hypothesized inferential mechanism fits the facts, one will provide added support for the hypothesized meaning which is held to underlie and to motivate the mechanism (cf. Kirsner, 1979:33–34, 186–187). Thus far, however, discussions of inferential mechanisms have been programmatic. By and large, they have been limited to demonstrations of the plausibility of a suggested mechanism, given relatively uncontroversial assumptions about human psychology (e.g., Reid, 1979).

The present paper constitutes an attempt to move from Task (1) toward Task (2). In what follows, both the meaning hypothesized for a particular form and the messages conveyed with that form will be held constant; that is, they themselves will not be open to discussion. We will be concerned instead with two alternative characterizations of the path from meaning to message. In earlier work, I considered these two characterizations to be equivalent: two different ways of saying the same thing. The present paper adopts a more critical stance and asks whether one of the proposed inferential mechanisms fits the available data better than the other, that is, provides a better picture of reality.

The particular problem under discussion is that of the Dutch "passive" and "pseudopassive," specifically the arguments made in Kirsner (1974, 1975, 1976a, 1976b) that these two uses of passive morphology are not separate units signaling separate meanings (as suggested by traditional grammar) but merely different exploitations of a single form–meaning complex. In previous work, I proposed a single meaning for passive morphology and presented two alternative inferential mechanisms to explain the greater tendency of the "pseudopassive" to refer to human actions (Kirsner, 1975:108–121, 1976a:11–14). In the present paper, I will evaluate the empirical adequacy of the two mechanisms in the light of quantitative observations on the occurrence of passive morphology in texts.

2. Case Study: The Dutch Passive[1]

2.1. The Traditional View

Traditional grammars of Dutch (e.g., den Hertog, 1973:162–163; Kruisinga, 1924:45) distinguish between so-called true passives such as (1) and so-called false passives, or pseudopassives, such as (2):

[1] This presentation of the problem draws on Kirsner (1975, 1976a).

(1)   a. *De huizen werden verwoest.*
         the houses became + destroyed
         'The houses were destroyed.'
      b. *De kaas werd gegeten.*
         the cheese became + eaten
         'The cheese was eaten."
(2)   a. *Er werd gefloten.*
         there became + whistled
         'There was whistling; someone whistled; people whistled.'
      b. *Er werd gegeten.*
         there became + eaten
         'There was eating; someone ate; people ate.'

The true passive and the pseudopassive differ as follows:

(3)   True passives   Pseudopassives
      a. Have an overt grammatical   a. Have no overt grammatical
         subject NP interpreted as a   subject NP whatsoever[2]
         logical object

      b. Cooccur with transitive and   b. Co-occur with intransitive
         pseudointransitive   verbs   and   pseudointransitive
         (i.e., verbs with omissible   verbs
         objects)

      c. Have an implied logical sub-   c. Have an implied logical sub-
         ject which may be human,   ject which is usually human
         nonhuman animate, or in-   and always animate
         animate

The essential contrast between true passive and pseudopassive is shown by
the pairs in (4) and (5):

(4)   a. *De* $\begin{Bmatrix} soldaat \\ wilde\ olifant \\ storm \end{Bmatrix}$ *verwoestte de huizen.*

         'The soldier/wild elephant/storm destroyed the houses.'

      b. *De huizen werden door de* $\begin{Bmatrix} soldaat \\ wilde\ olifant \\ storm \end{Bmatrix}$ *verwoest.*

         'The houses were destroyed by the soldier/wild elephant/storm.'

---

[2] For a discussion of why the adverbial *er* should not be considered a dummy NP, see Kirsner (1979). For a discussion of why it is unrewarding to consider *er* a "subject," see, in particular, Kirsner (1979:Chapter 9).

[239]

(5)   a. *De* $\begin{Bmatrix} jongen \\ vogel \\ fluitketel \end{Bmatrix}$ *floot.*

'The boy/bird/teakettle whistled.'

b. *Er werd door de* $\begin{Bmatrix} jongen \\ *vogel \\ *fluitketel \end{Bmatrix}$ *gefloten.*

'There was whistling by the boy/*bird/*teakettle.'

The transitive active sentences in (4a) each have a true passive counterpart in (4b). However, only that intransitive active sentence (5a) which has a HUMAN subject (namely, *de jongen* 'the boy') has a pseudopassive counterpart in (5b). This difference between the true passives in (4b) and the pseudopassives in (5b) raises the following important analytical question:

Is the restriction on the interpretation of passive morphology in the absence of a grammatical subject — that is, the restriction to (by and large) human activities or experiences — sufficient grounds for following the traditional grammarians and positing two separate passives in Dutch — a "true" passive and, entirely separate from it, a "false" one?

In earlier papers, I have answered this question in the negative and have argued that, in both its true and pseudopassive USES, Dutch passive morphology ITSELF is a single signal of a single meaning. In the following sections, I summarize my analysis and indicate the task it poses for the grammarian.

2.2. Overview of a Unitary Analysis

If one is to explain why passive morphology in Dutch has BOTH true AND pseudopassive uses, one cannot claim that it signals that the grammatical subject is logical object; the subjectLESS pseudopassive is an immediate counterexample.[3] One must instead observe what both uses have in common. Since in neither is the agent foregrounded as a grammatical subject (with which the verb "agrees" in number), one may reasonably hypothesize that THIS is what passive morphology itself asserts. Accordingly, I postulate that passive morphology in Dutch is the single signal of the single meaning HIGH PARTICIPANT NOT IN FOCUS.[4] By HIGH PARTICIPANT is meant a participant in the event named by the lexical verb which is comparatively

[3] It is the arbitrary acceptance of this sort of meaning as the only one possible for "passives" in all languages that leads grammarians such as Kruisinga (1924:45) to state that the pseudopassive in Dutch "expresses no passive meaning." See further Kirsner (1975:122–123).

[4] To avoid confusion with terminologies used in other schools of linguistics, I have replaced my earlier FOCUSED with IN FOCUS, in conformity with the text of Kirsner (1976a, 1979) as well as García (1975) and Zubin (1979).

high on a scale of relative activeness or contribution (cf. García, 1975:66–
68, 77–114; Zubin, 1977, 1979:474, Note 3). By IN FOCUS is meant in the
center of the speaker's interest[5] (cf. Kirsner, 1976b:388–390; 1979:92–95).
I use the term "passive morphology" to refer to the combination of either
the auxiliary verb *worden* 'become' or the auxiliary verb *zijn* 'be' plus the
past participle of the lexical verb (Kirsner, 1975:99, 1976a:5). (For discussion of the replacement of *worden* by *zijn* in perfect tenses, see Shetter,
1974:128–129.)

2.3. *Responsibilities of the Unitary Analysis*

It is not difficult to demonstrate that this analysis is consistent with both
the true passive and the pseudopassive uses of passive morphology. Consider once again Sentence (1a), *De huizen werden verwoest* 'The houses were
destroyed'. The plural ending *-en* on the auxiliary *worden* (here in the simple
preterite) signals the meaning THE PARTICIPANT IN FOCUS IS PLURAL (cf.
Kirsner, 1975:101, 1976a:6–8, 1979:92–98). Accordingly, it may be inferred that the plural NP *de huizen* is to be taken as the participant in focus,
that is, in the center of the speaker's interest (the subject). However, passive
morphology asserts HIGH PARTICIPANT NOT IN FOCUS. It follows (*a*) that the
houses, which are in focus, are NOT to be taken as relatively agentlike and (*b*)
that there is a second participant involved in the event which, though
unspecified here, IS more agentlike. We thus arrive at the traditionally
familiar true passive message that the participant in focus (subject) is a
nonagentlike entity in the event of destroying (hence a logical object).

Consider now Sentence (2a), *Er werd gefloten* 'There was whistling'. Here
again passive morphology tells us HIGH PARTICIPANT NOT IN FOCUS. However, there is no noun phrase which could be taken as referring to a
participant in focus. The auxiliary *worden* appears in the singular because
(*a*) some verb form must be there to indicate tense and (*b*) the third person
singular (cf. *Het regent* 'It is raining') is LESS INAPPROPRIATE than the third
person plural (cf. **Het regenen* 'It are raining') when there is in fact no
participant in focus.[6] But if there is no participant in focus, then the only

---

[5] The reader will observe that the use of the term "focus" within the analytical framework of this
paper (Form–Content analysis) differs from its use within other linguistic approaches (such as the
Extended Standard Theory of generative grammar); it may be very roughly paraphrased as "topicality
restricted to participants." Otheguy (1981) defines focus as "the speaker's concentration of attention
on one of the participants in the event [p. 11]." See, further, García (1975:68ff,184ff,233ff), Kirsner
(1979:92–95), and especially Zubin (1979).

[6] Given that there is in actuality no participant in the center of the speaker's interest, the meaning
THE PARTICIPANT IN FOCUS IS SINGULAR (signaled by the singular verb form) may be regarded as a
"lesser evil" than THE PARTICIPANT IN FOCUS IS PLURAL (signaled by the plural verb form), which
would suggest that not one but a multiplicity of entities are involved. See further Kirsner (1979:181)
and also the concept of the least inappropriate meaning (relative to a given message) in Kirsner
(1979:32–33).

[241]

participant mentioned at all is the agentlike entity referred to with the meaning HIGH PARTICIPANT NOT IN FOCUS. Given that this entity is high in contribution or activity, the event in question must be an action rather than a state. But because this participant is not in focus, it must be relatively backgrounded. The result is that the only thing emphasized (by default) is the action itself. We thus arrive at the typical pseudopassive message: 'There was VERBing'.

Notice, however, that is is not enough to demonstrate that the meaning HIGH PARTICIPANT NOT IN FOCUS is CONSISTENT with the pseudopassive as well as the true passive use. For the unitary analysis to be convincing, one must also be able to explain the greater tendency of the subjectless pseudo-passive to refer to human actions. Now, in a traditional analysis postulating separate true passive and pseudopassive units, one could do this simply by directly and explicitly attributing the difference in interpretation to the difference in meaning between the two units. In the present analysis, postulating no such difference in meaning, one must rely on the inferential process. What exactly is it about the absence of a participant in focus (subject) that favors the inference that the backgrounded high participant is human? In the following section we sketch two inferential mechanisms proposed in Kirsner (1975, 1976a) to account for this favoring.

3. Possible Explanations of the Inference 'Human Agent'

3.1. Mechanism A: Egocentricity and Inferential Complexity

Given that language is spoken by human beings, we may reasonably expect human abilities and interests to be reflected in language use. At least two general human characteristics appear to be responsible for the favoring by the pseudopassive of the inference of human agency: (*a*) egocentricity and (*b*) the avoidance of inferential complexity.

By egocentricity is meant the tendency to regard one's own experiences as inherently more noteworthy than those of others (Carnegie, 1963:60; James, 1950:289). Documented examples of the linguistic consequences of egocentricity include the interaction of case and person in Spanish (García, 1975:454–456) and the interaction of person and tense in both French (Reid, 1979:214–215) and German (Wolf, 1978:189–191). Particularly important for our understanding of the pseudopassive is Zubin's demonstration (1979:495–501) that the German nominative case (for which Zubin postulates the meaning FOCUS) is used most often to refer to the speaker and that the relative frequency of the nominative versus other cases decreases as one moves from speaker to other humans to inanimates and, finally, to abstractions. Data such as these, together with the purely psychological studies Zubin cites (1979:471–474), do much to convince one that, by and large, human beings do find themselves, and certainly other human beings, inherently more "interesting" than inanimate objects.

Consider now the second factor: the avoidance of inferential complexity.[7] Although it is true that human beings can jump to conclusions from sketchy data, it is to be expected that situations or events that are objectively less usual will be less easily and less readily inferred than those that are more normal in everyday experience. Someone seeing an old lady approach a door with a key in her hand will probably conclude that the lady intends to open the door with the key, not to use the key to carve her initials in the door, even though the latter event is at least possible (Kirsner, 1976a:4). The linguistic consequence of this state of affairs is that it should take more information—either more meanings and/or more precise meanings—to communicate a complicated or less obvious message than to communicate a simple one. Conversely, the fewer and/or less precise the meanings the speaker offers, the more likely the hearer should be to infer a "simple" or "obvious" message.[8]

Let us now examine the contrast between true passive and pseudopassive in the light of the preceding discussion. The first thing to note is that the true passive, containing a grammatical subject, offers the hearer more information than the pseudopassive does, and thereby favors to a greater extent the possibility of nontrivial inferences. The true passive contains a bona fide noun phrase which is taken as coreferential with the verb ending and which is characterized thereby as identifying the participant in focus: that entity, that participant, which is in the center of the speaker's interest. Because it depicts this participant as central, the true passive is naturally used to talk about it, to portray it as nonagentlike in the event. Consequently, whatever action the lexical verb names can be taken as important NOT in and of itself (as a "naturally" noteworthy activity) but only as an indication of the fate of the central participant, which remains in the spotlight. Although such actions often proceed from human beings (who are agents par excellence), they certainly need not do so in every case. Accordingly, the true passive may be used to refer to events in which the high participant is human or nonhuman, animate or inanimate.

---

[7] For a detailed discussion of this factor, see García (1975:Chapter 9).

[8] Consider the discussion of *My dog brought me my slippers, My wife brought me my slippers*, and *My wife brought me my slippers in her mouth* in Kirsner (1975:97–98, 1976a:4). As it is far more likely that the dog rather than the wife will bring the slippers by mouth, one must explicitly state that the wife uses her mouth if this unusual message is what one wishes to communicate.

The pseudopassive, on the other hand, backgrounds the high participant without foregrounding anything else. Indeed, the weak situational deixis provided by *er* 'unstressed there' only augments the defocusing of the agent which passive morphology signals (cf. Kirsner, 1979: Chapter 9). Accordingly, what is communicated is not the fate of some central participant but only the occurrence of an action. And almost by default, it is this action that is left in the spotlight. The question we may then ask is: What kind of actions are naturally egocentric human speakers likely to be interested in or find useful to talk about in and of themselves? Actions proceeding from humans or from nonhumans? Intuitively, the answer is "actions proceeding from humans." Given the paucity of information provided by the pseudopassive, that is indeed the most obvious, simplest inference possible.[9]

To summarize, Mechanism A would claim that the fact that the pseudopassive is interpreted more often than the true passive as referring to human actions follows directly from the absence of a grammatical subject specifying a participant in focus. When there is such a central participant in the event, the noteworthiness of the event can be attributed to it. When no central participant is mentioned, the event can be noteworthy only by virtue of the kind of action named. Egocentric human speakers will tend to find humans more interesting than nonhumans and actions caused by humans more noteworthy than actions caused by things. Accordingly, although both true and pseudopassives can refer to human actions, the tendency will be stronger in the latter.

3.2. Mechanism B: Strength of Backgrounding

A second way of explaining the greater tendency of the pseudopassive to refer to human actions is to propose an inferential mechanism based on the de facto strength with which the agent is removed from focus in the presence versus the absence of a grammatical subject. In both true passive and pseudopassive, passive morphology signals HIGH PARTICIPANT NOT IN FOCUS, thereby backgrounding the agent. Nevertheless, the degree of backgrounding differs. In the true passive, there is a foregrounded entity: the subject, the participant IN FOCUS in the event named by the verb. An implicit comparison is thus set up between one entity in focus and one out of

[9] Some cross-linguistic support for Mechanism A is provided by English sentences such as *There was whistling*, which communicate the occurrence of an action without mentioning the agent. Note, first, that such sentences contain very little information (Bolinger, 1975:244). Note, second, that they, too, are restricted to human actions: *There was hissing in the auditorium* is more acceptable than *There was hissing in the engine room*; *There was whispering by the second graders* is more acceptable than *There was whispering by the leaves* (cf. Kirsner, 1975:110). See also García (1975:200–204) on the inferential mechanisms underlying the "impersonal" use of *se* in Spanish.

focus. If the high (agentlike) participant is out of focus, it is so only with respect to the (nonagentlike) participant IN focus. The withdrawal of focus from the agent in the true passive is therefore qualified. It is only relative, analogous to the partial denial of height in the sentence *Compared to Bill, Tom is not tall.*

In the pseudopassive, by contrast, there is no foregrounded entity. When it is asserted that the high participant is not in focus, the resulting backgrounding is absolute, for it reflects only on the high participant itself. The withdrawal of focus from the agent in the pseudopassive is thus complete, analogous to the total denial of height in the sentence *Tom is not tall.*

Consider now that the meaning hypothesized for passive morphology contains a negative (HIGH PARTICIPANT NOT IN FOCUS) and that negatives in discourse typically communicate that the corresponding positive state of affairs has been held to be possible if not probable (cf. Wason, 1965; Givón, 1979:112). Accordingly, to signal HIGH PARTICIPANT NOT IN FOCUS is to suggest not only that agents typically are in focus (which is certainly true) but also that the particular agent being backgrounded is eligible for focus.[10] Now it is reasonable to assume that human speakers will consider humans inherently more focusworthy than animals or inanimates (cf. García, 1975:107; Zubin, 1979:495–497). Accordingly, use of HIGH PARTICIPANT NOT IN FOCUS, in either the true passive or pseudopassive, will suggest that the backgrounded agent is human. Nevertheless, because the negation of focus is more absolute in the pseudopassive, we would expect the suggestion of humanness to be stronger there.[11] And indeed it is.

3.3. The Nonequivalence of Mechanisms A and B

Though both inferential mechanisms aim to explain the same facts, they emphasize different things. Mechanism A takes the viewpoint of both speaker and hearer. It focuses on the communicative motivation of the true passive and pseudopassive in their entirety and asks for what different reasons a speaker might wish to talk about an event with a backgrounded agent when there is and when there is not some central participant. When there is one, it is this entity, the participant in focus, which motivates the use of passive morphology. When there is none, the activity itself is the motivator. The inference of human agency in both cases is presented globally: as "a

---

[10] Consider as an analogy the sentence *My daughter isn't married,* which suggests not only that woman marry but also that the daughter might be expected to be married and is therefore of marriageable age (eligible for marriage). Compare ???*My three-month-old daughter isn't married.*

[11] To continue with our analogy, compare *My daughter isn't married* with the emphatic *My daughter is NOT married AT ALL!* (cf. Kirsner, 1975:113, 1976a:13), suggesting greater prior expectation that the daughter was married.

sketchy appraisal of semantic [and pragmatic, RSK] probabilities, followed by a jump to the conclusion [García, 1975:43]." Its greater favoring in the pseudopassive is seen as resulting from the egocentricity of both speaker and hearer (so that both would be more interested in humans than anything else) plus the fact that the pseudopassive lacks the extra information about the nature of the event which a subject noun phrase could provide and which might help the hearer infer that the agent was not human.

Mechanism B is less direct, more analytical, and takes the viewpoint of the hearer only. Human agency is not so much "leapt at" as computed stepwise from the negation in HIGH PARTICIPANT NOT IN FOCUS (raising the question of the kind of entity which would have to have attention WITH-DRAWN from it) together with the presence or absence of a participant IN focus, which could serve as a potential yardstick of the "focusworthiness" of the backgrounded agent. (Is the agent backgrounded on its own merits or only by comparison to what is foregrounded?)

The interesting question that now arises is whether Mechanisms A and B can be distinguished empirically. If they are not merely different ways of saying the same thing (as originally suggested in Kirsner, 1975:122), then perhaps one can be shown to fit the empirical facts of Dutch usage better than the other.

4. Quantitative Hypotheses and Empirical Observations

4.1. *Predictions from Mechanism A*

If we assume that language users are in fact egocentric and do indeed avoid complex inferences, we may argue as follows. Because it is easier to infer that a backgrounded agent is human rather than nonhuman, speakers who wish to communicate a message in which the agent is nonhuman will have to help the hearer make a more difficult inference. In other words, as the situation being described is less likely, the speaker will have to provide the hearer with more information than would otherwise be the case. He will have to "spell out" more, by using either additional or more precise signal-meaning units. As shown in earlier examples, this "spelling out" can be achieved with a *door*-phrase, which specifies the agent explicitly — cf. Sentence (4b) *De huizen werden door de storm verwoest* 'the houses were destroyed by the storm.' Two predictions about such *door*-phrases immediately suggest themselves.

Consider first of all that (as Mechanism A attempts to explain) the inference of human agency is more favored in the pseudopassive. As the potential identity of the high participant is more restricted in the pseudo-

TABLE 1

Agent Expression in True and Pseudopassives[a]

AGENTIVE DOOR-PHRASE	TRUE PASSIVE (WITH SUBJECT)	PSEUDOPASSIVE (WITHOUT SUBJECT)	TOTAL
Present	38 (16%)	1 (3%)	39 (14%)
Absent	196 (84%)	39 (97%)	235 (86%)
	234	40	274

$$\chi^2(df = 1) = 4.217, p < .05$$

[a] Data from Kirsner (1976b:394).

passive than in the true passive (namely, to animates and humans), *door*-phrases should be less necessary and hence somewhat less frequent in the former than in the latter.

A second prediction concerns true passives alone. If *door*-phrases are used only when their "extra" information is needed, one should be able to observe a difference in true passives between agents whose identity is explicitly specified with a *door*-phrase and those whose identity is left to be inferred from context. By and large, the unspecified agents should tend to be human more frequently than the explicitly specified ones.

It should perhaps be emphasized at this point that predictions such as these cannot be adequately tested by casually asking a few native speakers for their intuitions. Both true passives and pseudopassives can occur both with and without *door*-phrases; in true passives, *door*-phrases can refer to humans and to nonhumans [cf. Section 2, Sentences in (4b)].[12] What we must do is examine not opinions about Dutch usage but that usage itself, in discourse, that is, in actual communication.

I have chosen as my initial corpus four connected texts: three novellas by Haasse, Hermans, and Reve plus a novelization of a film scenario by De Jong (cf. Kirsner, 1975:117, 1976b:392). Tables 1 and 2 give, respectively, the data relevant to the first and second predictions. The 38 full true passives (with agentive *door*-phrases) and the 196 agentless true passives (without *door*-phrases) that are examined in Table 2 are the same ones that are compared with pseudopassives in Table 1.

[12] That this is not possible in pseudopassives was pointed out in Section 2. For a discussion of why this is the case (which would go beyond the bounds of the present paper), the reader is referred to Kirsner (1976a:14–16). In terms of Mechanism A, such sentences as *Er werd door de fluitketel gefloten* 'There was whistling by the teapot' represent the ultimate in inferential complexity and pragmatic unlikelihood. As inanimates are inherently less focusworthy than humans to begin with, it would be relatively incoherent to first background them with passive morphology and then mention them in a *door*-phrase. If they are ineligible for the foreground, why do they have to be backgrounded? Once they are backgrounded, why mention them? The suggestion that the kind of whistling in question is important enough to be mentioned in and of itself collides with the specification of the high participant as inanimate.

TABLE 2
Type of Agent in the True Passives

	HUMAN	NONHUMAN	TOTAL
Full	20 (53%)	18 (47%)	38
Agentless	178 (91%)	18 (9%)	196

$\chi^2(df = 1) = 32.78, p < .0001$

It will be seen that both predictions are confirmed. Whereas 16% of the true passives in Table 1 contained agentive *door*-phrases, only 3% of the pseudopassives did — a skewing which could occur by chance less than 1 time out of 20, according to the chi square test. A closer look at the true passives, in turn, showed that, in the absence of a *door*-phrase, the high participant could be inferred from the context to be human 91% of the time. When, however, an explicit *door*-phrase was present, the high participant was specified as human only 53% of the time. This skewing, too, is highly significant; its probability of occurring by chance is less than 1 in 10,000.

4.2. *Predictions from Mechanism B*

Consider now the empirical predictions one could make from mechanism B rather than A. According to B, the pseudopassive favors the inference of human agency more than the true passive does because it withdraws focus more strongly from the high participant, backgrounding it more forcibly. The reason for this greater backgrounding is held to be that the presence of a grammatical subject, referring to a particular participant IN FOCUS, automatically provides a specific basis of comparison with what is OUT OF FOCUS. It is as if the pseudopassive says "High participant out of focus" but the true passive says "Compared to this particular participant in focus, the high participant is out of focus." The backgrounding in the latter case is relative rather than absolute.

Suppose now that there were some objective measure of the actual degree of backgrounding of the high participant in Dutch sentences containing passive morphology. If there were, we should be able to observe that backgrounding was indeed higher in the pseudopassive than in the true passive. We should also be able to detect several other things, as follows.

Recall that, according to Mechanism B, the backgrounding of the agent in the true passive is relative and therefore potentially variable. By this reasoning, if the high participant is out of focus only by comparison to the subject, then different kinds of subjects should cause this participant to be backgrounded to different degrees. Furthermore, it would seem that the subject, referring to a participant in focus, would act as an "upper bound" with respect to the out of focus agent, so that the agent would at least never be more foregrounded than the subject was. Finally, it follows that if we could manipulate the degree of foregrounding on the subject, we could also manipulate the degree of backgrounding on the agent; the out of focus agent would always be more backgrounded (on some absolute scale of messages) than the in focus subject. And the more foregounded the subject (on this absolute scale), the more foregrounded — and hence the less backgrounded — the agent would be. Hence, if we could objectively measure in true passives both subject foregrounding and agent backgrounding, we should find an inverse correlation between the two: The more foregrounded the subject, the less backgrounded the agent.

As suggested in Kirsner (1976b:393), one plausible measure of the de facto degree of foregrounding of the subject (the extent to which it is already in the center of attention) is the degree of anaphoricity of the noun phrase referring to it (cf. Cole, 1974). By and large, a definite NP will indicate greater foregrounding than a plain indefinite NP which, in turn, will indicate greater foregrounding than an *er*-introduced indefinite NP (cf. Kirsner, 1976b:412, Note 8):

(6)

		Degree of subject foregrounding
a.	*De liedjes werden gezongen.* 'The songs were sung.'	high
b.	*Liedjes werden gezongen.* 'Songs were sung.'	medium
c.	*Er werden liedjes gezongen.* 'There were songs sung.'	low

Consequently, one way to test Mechanism B would be to examine agent backgrounding in true passives as a function of subject type. If our argument thus far is correct, we would expect to find the least backgrounding of agents in sentences with the most anaphoric subjects (definite NPs), more backgrounding in sentences with plain indefinite subjects, and maximum backgrounding in sentences with the least anaphoric subjects: *er*-introduced indefinite NPs in so-called presentative sentences. Additionally, we might expect this last type of true passive to be most similar to pseudopassives, in which there is no subject NP at all and agent backgrounding is held to be strongest. There should thus be a CONTINUUM of agent backgrounding with a maximum at pseudopassives (*Er werd gezongen* 'There was singing'), a lessening through sentences like (6c) *Er werden liedjes gezongen* and (6b) *Liedjes werden gezongen,* and finally a minimum at (6a) *De liedjes werden gezongen* 'The songs were sung'.

The only problem now remaining is to find an objective measure of agent backgrounding. One possibility might be the frequency with which the agent is explicitly specified in a *door*-phrase in sentences with the different subject types. Recall that passive morphology signals HIGH PARTICIPANT NOT IN FOCUS, withdrawing the agent from attention. Now, if the agent were truly being backgrounded, explicit mention of it in a prepositional phrase would only increase the attention on the agent and should be — by and large — relatively incoherent, that is, inconsistent with backgrounding. Moreover, the greater the degree of backgrounding, the greater we would expect the incoherence to be and the more it should be avoided.

Accordingly, if Mechanism B and the preceding argument are correct, we may predict the following:

1. The frequency of agentive prepositional phrases should be lower in pseudopassives than in true passives.
2. Furthermore, the frequency of agentive prepositional phrases should drop monotonically as one moves from true passives with definite subjects to those with plain indefinite subjects, then to those with *er*-introduced indefinite subjects and, finally, to pseudopassives. This second prediction is diagrammed in Figure 1.

The reader will observe that Prediction (1) from Mechanism B is exactly the same as the first prediction from Mechanism A, given in Section 4.1. Supporting data have already been presented in Table 1. As the same facts are predicted from both mechanisms, Prediction (1) does not allow us to decide that one mechanism is "truer" than the other.

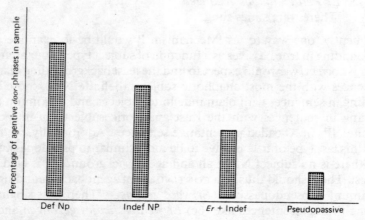

FIGURE 1. Predicted relationship of *door*-phrase frequency to subject type according to Mechanism B.

TABLE 3
Agent Expression by Subject Type[a]

SUBJECT TYPE: PASSIVE TYPE:	1 DEF NP TRUE	2 INDEF NP TRUE	3 ER + INDEF TRUE	4 ABSENT PSEUDO	5 INDETERMINATE TRUE
door-Phrase					
Present	32 (21%)	3 (13%)	0 (0%)	1 (3%)	3 (9%)
Absent	123	20	24	39	29
Total	155	23	24	40	32

[a] Data from Kirsner (1976b:394).

Table 3 divides the data from Table 1 according to subject type, in order to test Prediction 2. Note that I have had to set up a new category of true passives called "indeterminate", to the right of the others, for those true passives whose subjects could not be unambiguously ranked on the anaphoricity scale.[13] This column will be excluded from subsequent calculations.

At first glance it looks as though the hypothesis is confirmed, for as one goes from definite subjects in Column 1 to plain indefinites in Column 2, and so forth, the percentage of *door*-phrases drops from 21% to 13% to 0%. And the 3% for pseudopassives in Column 4 may well represent a fluctuation due to small sample size: 0/24 is not essentially different from 1/40. Nevertheless, before drawing conclusions from these data, we must determine whether they are significant.

If we cast the data from Columns 1–4 into a single 2 × 4 table, it is clear that there is some sort of gross association of *door*-phrases with more anaphoric subjects: $\chi^2(df = 3) = 13.17$, $p < .005$. However, if we partition this 2 × 4 table into a series of 2 × 2 tables, as discussed in Maxwell (1961:Chapter 3),[14] we discover that the only significant difference in the frequency of *door*-phrases is between true passives with definite NP subjects (Column 1: 21% *door*-phrases) and all the rest (Columns 2, 3, and 4 lumped together: 5% *door*-phrases). For this 2 × 2 table, we find $\chi^2(df = 1) = 10.10$, $p < .002$. There is no difference between the frequency of *door*-phrases in

[13] These include relative pronoun subjects, gapped subjects, and the like. Because they are all true passives, we expect the frequency of agentive *door*-phrases in them to be higher than in pseudopassives. However, as I could not decide where to put them on the anaphoricity scale, I thought it best to exclude them from the test of the hypothesis that the frequency of *door*-phrases correlates with subject anaphoricity/presence.

[14] Maxwell (1961:52) describes this as "partitioning the degrees of freedom on which the overall [chi-square] value is based" and "subdivision of the overall chi-square value into additive components."

Column 2 (plain indefinite subjects), Column 3 (*er*-introduced indefinite subjects), and Column 4 (pseudopassives with no subject). Hence, we must conclude that although there is some trend in the data, there is not sufficient evidence for the orderly monotonic decrease in *door*-phrase frequency which had been predicted.

It might now be suggested that the reason this prediction was not confirmed was that the sample size was simply too small. In addition, it may be argued that passive sentences from literary texts alone are not necessarily representative of Dutch usage (cf. Gielen, 1979:37). Accordingly, it will be useful to examine other passive sentences, from a different genre. Table 4 below presents additional data[15] from random fragments of newspaper Dutch used in a study of word frequency (Uit den Boogaart, 1975). The total number of sentences counted is 803 (versus 274 in Table 3).

Note first that we find exactly the same pattern as before: a drop from 21% in Column 1 to 9% to 3% and then a slight rise to 8%. Again, the 2 × 4 table (for Columns 1–4) shows a significant overall trend in the data: $\chi^2(df = 3) = 19.09$, $p < .001$. However, when we partition this overall chi square value into components, we find again that the overall trend is entirely due to the difference between Column 1 (21% *door*-phrases) and Columns 2, 3, 4 and taken together (8% *door*-phrases); $\chi^2(df = 1) = 17.26$, $p < .0001$. There is no significant difference in the frequency of *door*-phrases in Columns 2, 3, and 4, and thus there is again no evidence for an orderly decrease in *door*-phrase frequency.

TABLE 4.
Agent Expression by Subject Type[a]

SUBJECT TYPE: PASSIVE TYPE:	1 DEF NP TRUE	2 INDEF NP TRUE	3 ER + INDEF TRUE	4 ABSENT PSEUDO	5 INDETERMINATE TRUE
door-Phrase					
Present	80 (21%)	14 (9%)	1 (3%)	5 (8%)	19 (12%)
Absent	309	137	34	59	145
Total	389	151	35	64	164

[a] Data from Uit den Boogaart, 1975, Corpus 1.

[15] The 803 passive sentences counted here were retrieved by hand from a listing of all sentences in Corpus 1 (Newspapers) in the Uit den Boogaart collection which contained any present tense, past tense, or infinitive form of the verb *worden* 'become'. I am grateful to ir. G. J. van der Steen of the Computer Division, Faculty of Letters, University of Amsterdam, for providing me with this listing. Unfortunately, the coding used in the Uit den Boogaart corpora did not allow retrieval of passive sentences as such (cf. the discussion in Renkema, 1981). The present sample—only a subset of the passives in Corpus 1—does not include passive sentences in perfect tenses, as in these the auxiliary verb is not *worden* but *zijn* (Shetter, 1974:128).

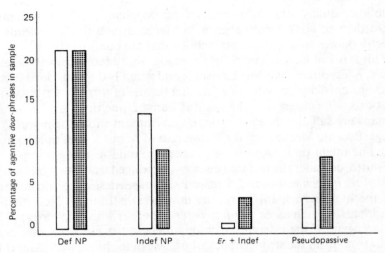

FIGURE 2. Observed relationship of *door*-phrase frequency to subject type in data from Kirsner (1976b) [white] and Uit den Boogaart (1975) [black].

Figure 2 displays the parallel trends exhibited by the data in Tables 3 and 4.

Because nothing in Mechanism B suggests that there will be a crucial difference between the use of passive morphology in literary texts and in newspapers, we might wish to increase the sample size yet again by pooling Tables 3 and 4, especially given the parallelism between the data sets.[16] Doing so yields no new result; the only significant difference in *door*-phrase frequency remains that between true passives with definite subjects (Column 1) and all others (Columns 2, 3, and 4).

5. Discussion

There are several points that can now be made about the relative merits of Mechanisms A and B. The first is that whereas both predictions from A are confirmed by the data, only one prediction from B is—the same one that also follows from A (data in Table 1).

A second point is that, on the basis of Mechanism A, one can make a second prediction which is confirmed by the data (namely, the prediction concerning the humanness of the high participant) but which does not seem

[16] George Mount has pointed out to me that approximately 97% of the variance among the paired data values is linear and that one can reasonably assume that the agreement between the two samples is not due to chance.

Robert S. Kirsner

to follow equally straightforwardly from Mechanism B.[17] Mechanism A might then be considered superior to Mechanism B in that it leads more directly than B to just those predictions that are confirmed.

Third, it will have occurred to the reader that Mechanism B, taken as a whole, is less direct than Mechanism A and actually depends on at least part of A: egocentricity. In order to argue that the use of HIGH PARTICIPANT NOT IN FOCUS will suggest that the agent is human, one must first assume that humans are sufficiently egocentric to find humans more focusworthy than things. Because Mechanism B requires part of A, but A does not require any of B, one might prefer A to B on internal grounds, as being "simpler."

Fourth, consider the fact that even *er*-introduced true passives, such as *Er werden zes huizen verwoest* 'There were six houses destroyed', do not suggest that the high participant (here: the destroyer) is human. Nevertheless, a pseudopassive such as *Er wordt gefloten* 'There is whistling' does suggest a human agent. If the inference of humanness in the pseudopassive is to be EXPLAINED from the stronger backgrounding of the high participant (Mechanism B), then there should be tangible evidence that pseudopassives do in fact background that participant more forcefully than *er*-introduced true passives. But there is none, at least not with the measure we have used. No significant difference in *door*-phrase frequency was observed between Columns 3 and 4 in Table 3, Table 4, or a fifth table with the data pooled from the previous two. Indeed, in all three tables, Column 4 shows a slight rise when compared to Column 3.

A final point is that the favoring of *door*-phrases by true passives with definite subjects might have less to do with the variable backgrounding of the agent than with a more general tendency for additional participants in an event to be mentioned only when there is a participant in focus (subject) that is fully foregrounded. Kirsner (1979:151) presents data on ACTIVE sentences showing a direct correlation between the anaphoricity of the subject NP and the presence of one or more "bare" object NPs. The relative frequency of such sentences as *De jongen heeft een steen gegooid* 'The boy threw a stone' within the category of sentences with definite subjects is higher than that of sentences like *Een jongen heeft een steen gegooid* 'A boy threw a stone' within the category of sentences with plain indefinite subjects. Similarly, the relative frequency of sentences like *Een jongen heeft een steen gegooid* is higher than that of sentences such as *Er heeft een jongen een steen gegooid* 'There threw a boy a stone' within the category of sentences with *er*-introduced indefinite subjects. Whereas 46% of the sentences with definite subjects contain objects, only 13% of the sentences with plain indefinite

[17] It is not clear to me at this writing how one could derive the second prediction from Mechanism A on the basis of Mechanism B instead.

[254]

subjects do. The fraction of sentences with *er*-introduced indefinite subjects that contain objects is still lower: 1%. To the extent that both a *door*-phrase in a passive sentence and a bare object NP in an active sentence mention some additional entity other than the participant in focus, there is a rough parallelism between this trend and the data in Tables 3 and 4. Given that the second prediction made by Mechanism B (monotonic decrease in *door*-phrase frequency) was not confirmed, and given that an alternative explanation might be available for the "degenerate" trend which WAS observed, support for Mechanism B is lessened.

On balance, then, it would seem that an inferential mechanism based on human egocentricity and the human avoidance of less probable, complex inferences is somewhat more credible than one based on the degree of backgrounding of the agent in different passive sentence types. Mechanism A is conceptually simpler than B and leads to two straightforward "common sense" predictions which are cleanly confirmed by the data. Mechanism B (more complicated in that it needs A's concept of egocentricity) leads to a prediction that is not cleanly confirmed, even when the sample size is more than tripled. (Indeed, the "degenerate" data which are observed might well be explained from a more general principle relating subject type and the number of arguments to the verb in active sentences as well as passives.) Finally, although both A and B predict that *door*-phrases will be more frequent in true passives than in pseudopassives, it is not clear how one could coherently deduce from B that nonstated agents will be human more often than agents explicitly mentioned in *door*-phrases.

6. Conclusion

In this paper, we have utilized quantitative data from discourse (literary texts and newspapers) to evaluate two alternative inferential mechanisms which have been proposed as part of a unitary analysis of the Dutch passive. To the extent that predictions based on one mechanism are confirmed more neatly than those based on the other, we would suggest that one gives more insight into the way Dutch passive morphology is actually exploited in communication. And, to the extent that this mechanism requires the postulation of one single meaning for passive morphology in both the true passive and pseudopassive use, acceptance of the mechanism entails acceptance of the unitary analysis as well.

It will be seen, then, that the entire argument is grounded in the discourse data. The postulation of a signal-meaning unit to explain the otherwise mysterious correlations between morphology and messages must be complemented by the postulation of meaning-dependent inferential mechanisms. These, in turn, must be tested — not unempirically, against artificial intuitions or scattered opinions about what one "might" say and what it "could" mean, but empirically, against the natural functioning of language in discourse: as an instrument of human communication.

Acknowledgments

The research discussed here was supported by grant 2964 from the University of California, Los Angeles Academic Senate. I wish to thank Ellen Contini-Morava, Erica García, Vincent van Heuven, George E. Mount, Wallis H. Reid, and Mel Widawski for their useful and detailed criticism of earlier versions of this paper.

References

Bolinger, D. 1975. *Aspects of language.* New York: Harcourt Brace Jovanovich.

Carnegie, D. 1963. *How to win friends and influence people.* New York: Pocket Books.

Cole, P. 1974. Indefiniteness and anaphoricity. *Language* 50, 665–674.

Diver, W. 1981. On defining the discipline. *Columbia University Working Papers in Linguistics* 6, 59–117.

García, E. 1975. *The role of theory in linguistic analysis: the Spanish pronoun system.* Amsterdam: North-Holland.

Gielen, P. 1979. *Onpersoonlijk passief in het Nederlands en enkele andere constructies met er.* Doctoraalscriptie, Instituut voor Algemene Taalwetenschap, Universiteit van Amsterdam.

Givón, T. 1979. *On understanding grammar.* New York: Academic Press.

Hertog, C. den 1973. *Nederlandse spraakkunst,* vol. 3. *De leer van de woordsoorten.* H. Hulshof (Ed.). Amsterdam: W. Versluys.

James, W. 1950. *The principles of psychology,* vol. 1. New York: Dover.

Kirsner, R. S. 1974. On pragmatic inference and communicative strategies: the problem of the Dutch 'pseudo-passive.' Paper presented at the annual meeting of the Linguistic Society of America, New York, New York.

Kirsner, R. S. 1975. On the mechanism of the restriction of the Dutch 'pseudopassive' to human actions. *Columbia University Working Papers in Linguistics* 2. (Second, corrected printing, 1980, pp. 93–125.)

Kirsner, R. S. 1976a. De 'onechte lijdende vorm.' *Spektator* 6, 1–18.

Kirsner, R. S. 1976b. On the subjectless 'pseudo-passive' in Standard Dutch and the semantics of background agents. In C. Li (Ed.), *Subject and topic.* New York: Academic Press.

Kirsner, R. S. 1979. *The problem of presentative sentences in Modern Dutch.* Amsterdam: North-Holland.

Kruisinga, E. 1924. *A grammar of Modern Dutch.* London: Allen & Unwin.

Maxwell, A. E. 1961. *Analysing qualitative data.* London: Methuen.

Otheguy, R. 1981. *Tout se tient:* Deixis, focus, and degree of participation in Spanish. *Columbia University Working Papers in Linguistics* 6, 1–44.

Reid, W. 1979. *The human factor in linguistic analysis: The passé simple and the imparfait.* Unpublished doctoral dissertation, Columbia University.

Renkema, J. 1981. *De taal van 'Den Haag.' Een kwantitatief–stilistisch onderzoek naar aanleiding van oordelen over taalgebruik.* 's-Gravenhage: Staatsuitgeverij.

Shetter, W. 1974. *Introduction to Dutch.* The Hague: Martinus Nijhoff.

Uit den Boogaart, P. C. (Ed.). 1975. *Woordfrequenties in geschreven en gesproken Nederlands.* Utrecht: Oosthoek, Scheltema & Holkema.

Wason, P. C. 1965. The contexts of plausible denial. *Journal of Verbal Learning and Verbal Behavior* 4, 7–11.

Wolf, H. 1978. *The semantics of tense in Modern German.* Unpublished doctoral dissertation, University of California, Los Angeles.

Zubin, D. A. 1977. The semantic basis of case alternation in German. In R. Fasold and R. Shuy (Eds.), *Studies in language variation.* Washington, D.C.: Georgetown University Press.

Zubin, D. A. 1979. Discourse function of morphology: the focus system in German. In T. Givón (Ed.), *Syntax and semantics, vol. 12.* New York: Academic Press.